Rest

by C.J. Lovik

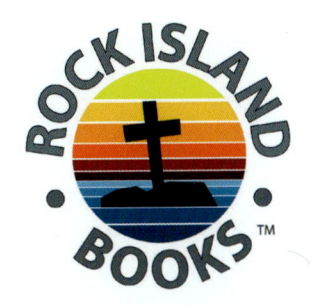

www.rockislandbooks.com
Visit our website to purchase books and preview upcoming titles.

Contact us at:
books@rockisland.com

*Copyright © 2015, C.J. Lovik
All rights reserved*

*To my dear friends
Buck and Susan Keely,
whose lives and love for the
Gospel have been an
inspiration to me
and my family.*

Contents

Introduction – page 5

Chapter 1: The end of evil and the end of grace – page 7

Chapter 2: Perfection, and the five principles underlying Everlasting Rest – page 15

Chapter 3: Enjoyment of God and those who fear it – page 23

Chapter 4: Digging holes, a parable – page 31

Chapter 5: The nature of rest and the foundation of the promise – page 37

Chapter 6: With me or without me. The paradox of burden – page 43

Chapter 7: The difficult path that leads to Rest, and what must be left behind – page 49

Chapter 8: When evil can no longer torment or threaten you – page 55

Chapter 9: Heaven. A place to remember – page 69

About the author – page 84

Cover illustration by JoAnn Lovik

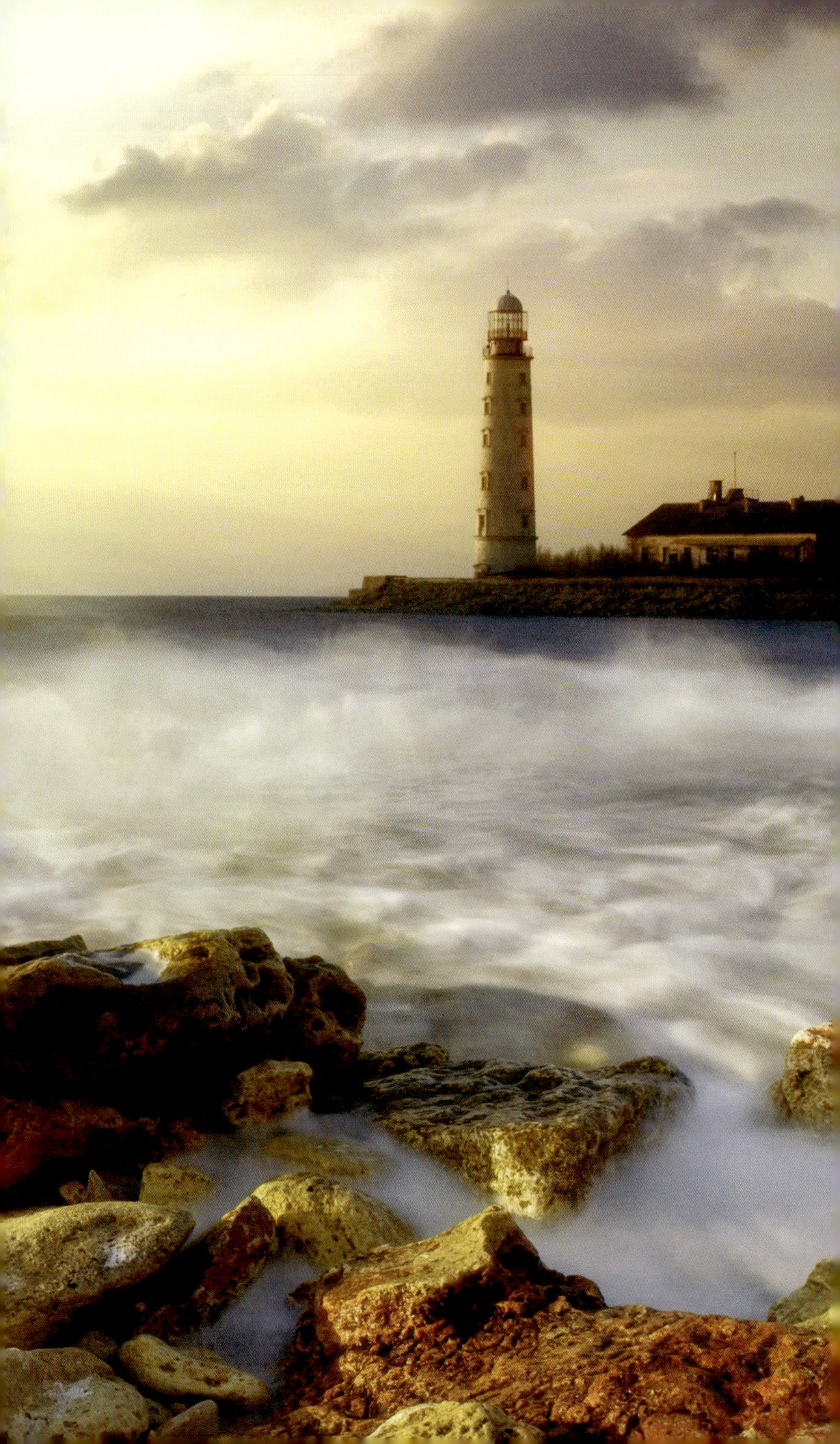

Introduction

THE Saints Everlasting Rest by Richard Baxter stands alone as one of the stellar witnesses to the reality and ultimate motivations for treading the pilgrim path in order to arrive safely in Heaven's Rest.

Unfortunately it is not widely read today. One of the reasons this amazing book is rarely read by Christians is because it is dated and difficult for most people to read.

It is with this in mind that I offer an original rendering inspired by the first chapter of *The Saints Everlasting Rest.*

The book you are about to read is original with me. It is not a paraphrase or translation, but it does build on the outline of the book originally written by Baxter. I have also included a few inspirational quotes by Baxter.

So while this book is original with the author, it owes its rebirth to Baxter. This is a work launched by one saint and now rewritten for another generation in order to reveal the timeless truths of Scripture.

May you be blessed and encouraged as you read this short book.

– C.J. Lovik

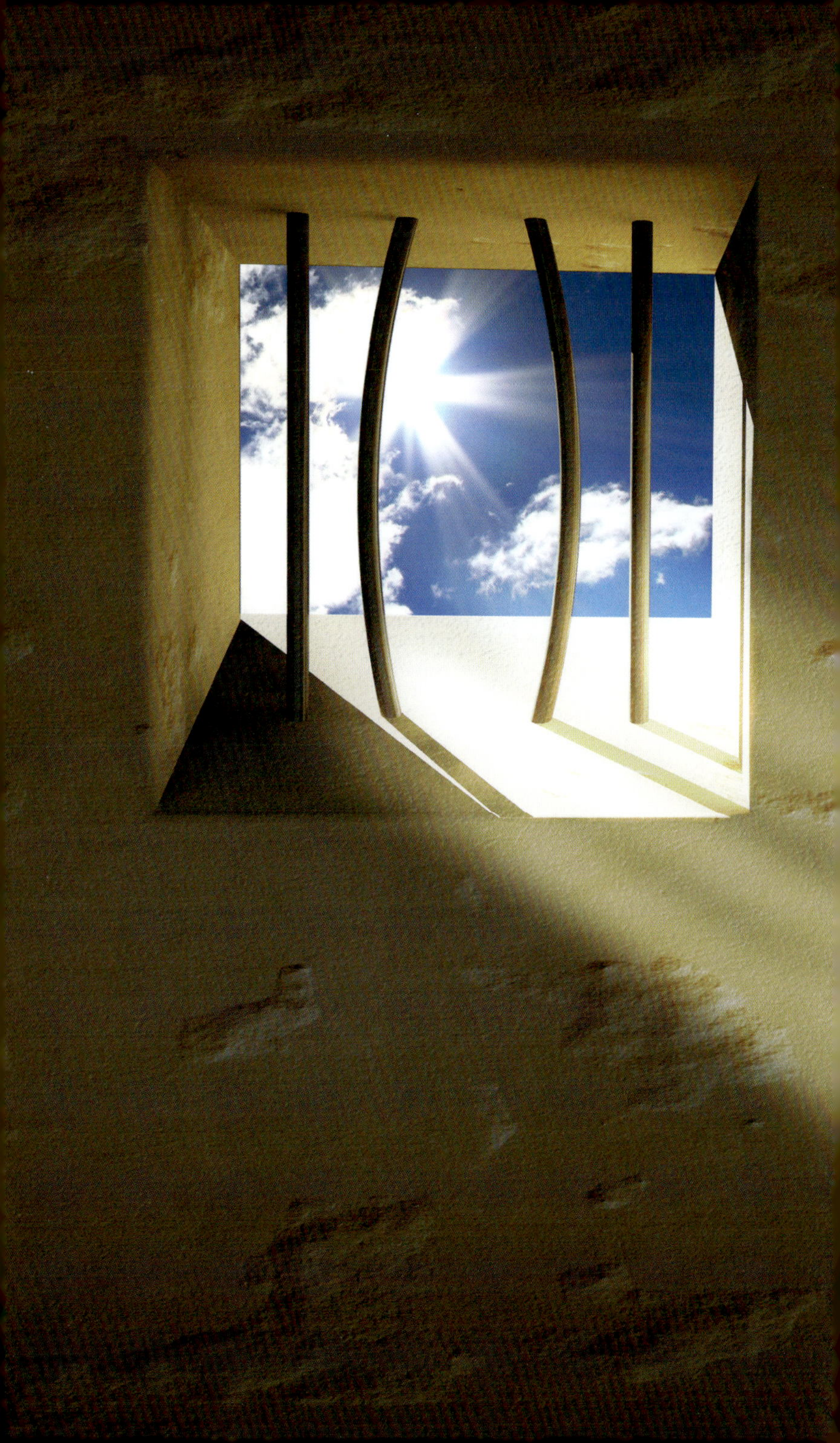

Chapter 1

The end of evil
. . .and the end of grace

Hebrews 4:9-10
There remaineth therefore a rest to the people of God. For he that is entered into his rest, he also hath ceased from his own works, as God did from his.

I cannot fully comprehend the complete meaning of the "rest" that Apostle Paul speaks of in his letter to the Hebrews.

Nevertheless we may nibble around the edges of this sweet manna that has come to us from Heaven by God's intentional, if not fully illuminated, revelation.

What does it speak to the soul? What does it say to one who has found genuine, but mostly unrealized, rest in the work of Christ's Cross?

Rest! What is this "rest" that Jesus proclaims as he beckons those who are weary and burdened to come to him and receive? (Matthew 11:26)

Something comes to an end just before this most anticipated rest is completely and fully realized. Do you know what it is? It may surprise you!

A STORY OF GRACE

The bucket quickly swished up the creek water and captured a small fry moments before it would be swallowed by a larger trout.

Joshua, who scooped up the fingerling, decided that he would keep it alive and transport it to the pond in his back yard, a couple miles away.

Joshua's rescue plan posed two challenges. The first was that the bucket he used to capture the trout had a leak.

The second problem was that all the bouncing up and down in the back of his dad's pickup truck would surely slosh all the water out of the bucket before they reached home. What to do?

Joshua thought about the problem and came up with a solution. He filled his lunch thermos with creek water and carefully positioned himself with his bucket and wiggling passenger in the bed of his dad's pickup.

Joshua pressed the bucket between his knees as the old truck rumbled down the bumpy dirt road. He found himself fully engaged in preventing water from sloshing out of the bucket and, at the same time, adding water as needed.

The two-mile journey seemed an eternity, but Joshua and his small trophy arrived safely home. It took Joshua only a minute to take the bucket down to the pond and gently pour the agitated trout into its new nursery.

WHEN GRACE IS NO LONGER NECESSARY

This very imperfect illustration does manage to teach a lesson in grace.

While the first act of grace was evident in the rescuing of the small trout, the second act of grace was achieved not by one work, but by many means. The constant resupplying of the water, the balancing of the bucket, the quick hands preventing the life-giving water from escaping the bucket.

When the trout left the confines of the bucket and entered the five-acre pond, the means of grace ended for the small fish.

> When we enter God's final rest, the means of grace cease, as they are no longer necessary.

The angels who had been assigned to preserve our welfare report for new duties. All the circumstances that God surrounded us with to keep us from destroying ourselves immediately cease.

It is only God's preserving and enabling Spirit, and the good intentions of God for you, and the ever vigilant persevering hand of the Savior that has kept us from sliding down the hill upon which the Savior's cross stands as our only hope.

Once begun, the slide down is not inconsequential. The welcoming, often-traveled path tumbles down to an irretrievable entrance into a grave, which is the doorway to an eternal Hell.

In a word, if all means of God's good grace end, and I am now to enter a place of perfection, I have a real dilemma.

To put it plainly, I am unfit for the place and could never hope to enter into its sanctuary without some intervening miracle.

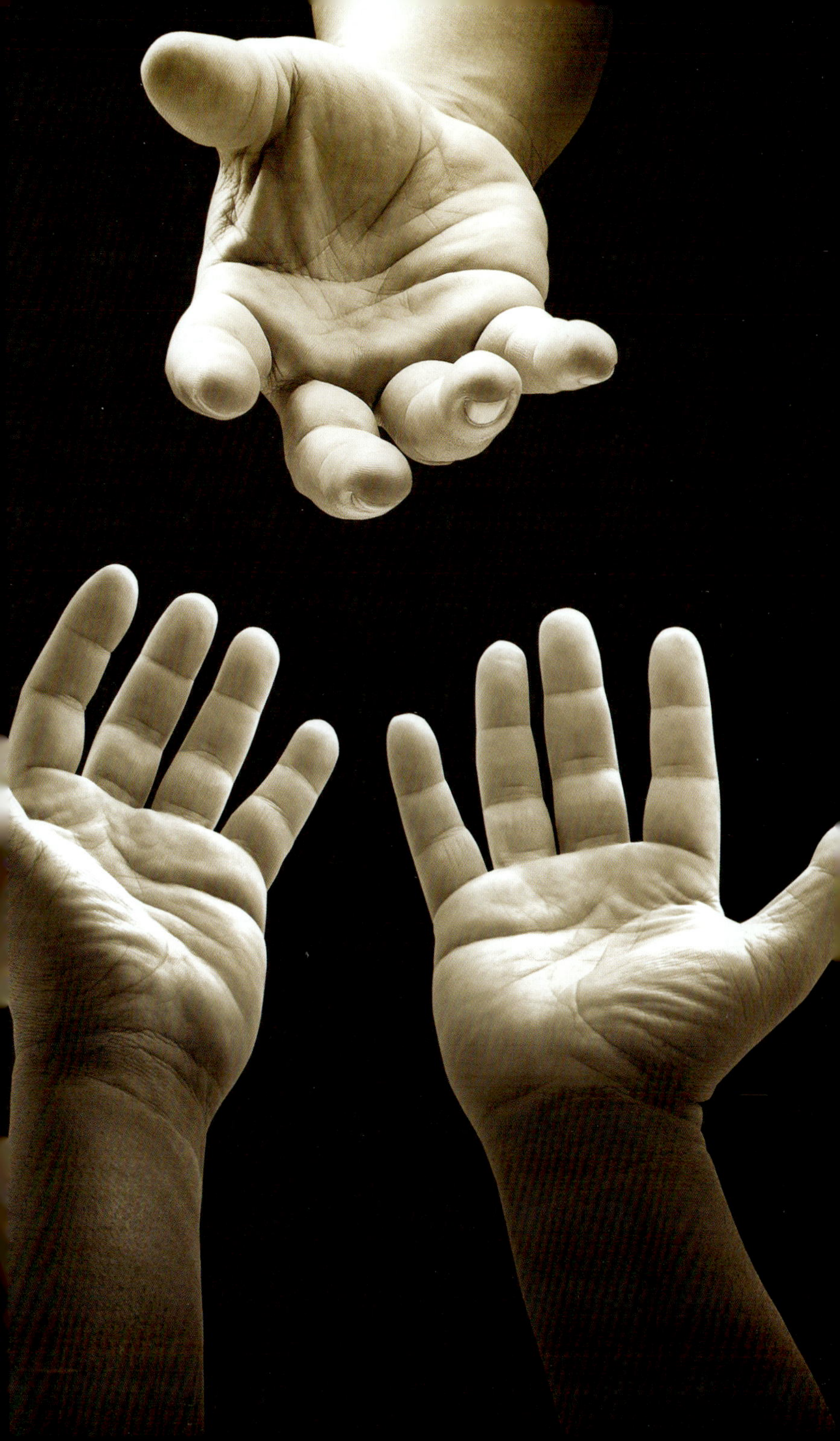

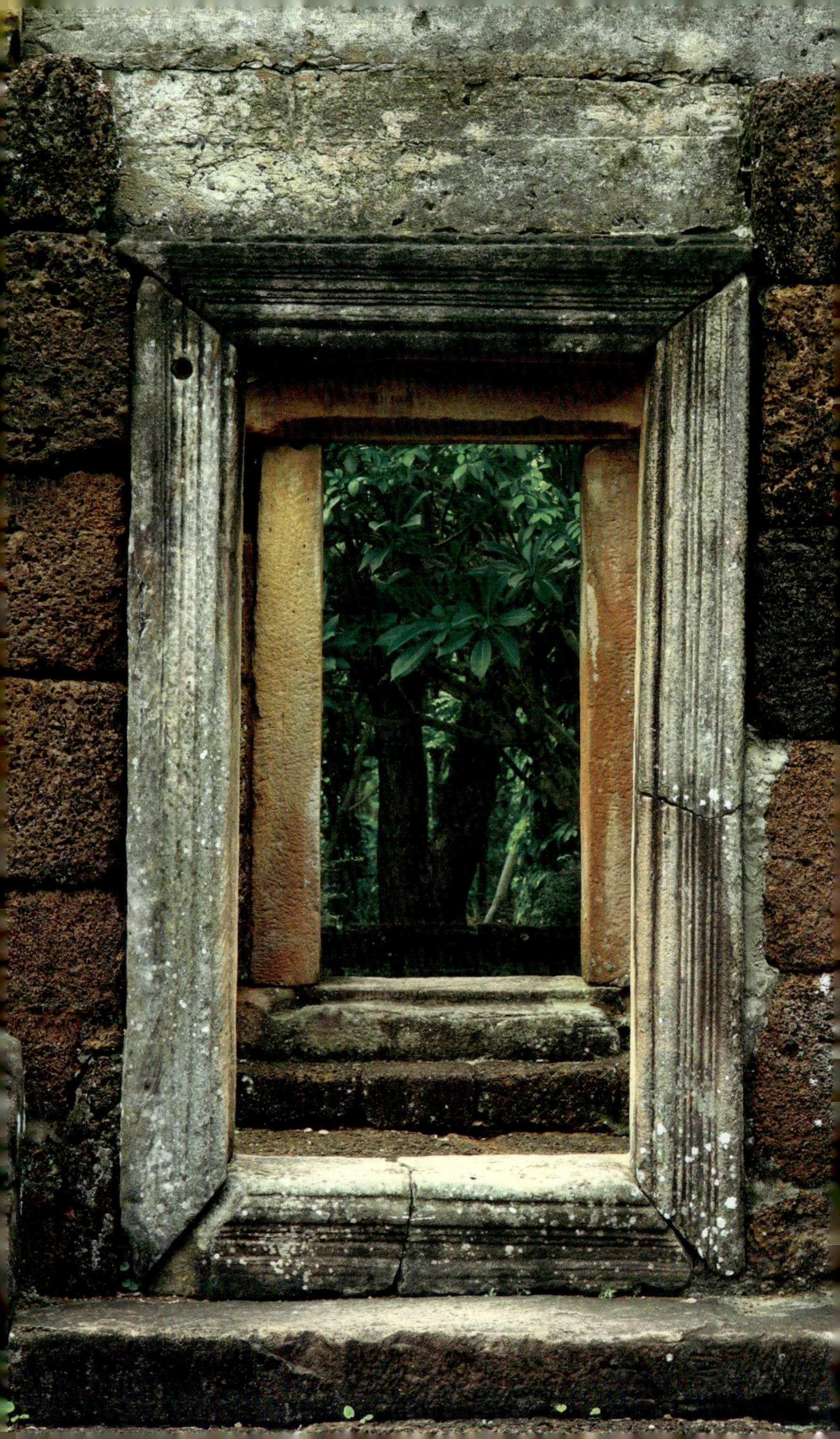

Chapter 2

Perfection

...and the five principles underlying Everlasting Rest

THERE is *good news* for sinners! We are to be thoroughly and completely perfected in body and our soul.

Let that sink in for a moment. You will be changed so as to fit perfectly into a perfect Heaven. And this does not happen haphazardly or without great design. It is in point of fact a change that requires the highest degree of skill and exquisite workmanship. And who is given this task?

> Is it an angel trained in human transformation?
>
> Perhaps a group of Heaven's best tutors are sent to educate you in the etiquette of heavenly manners and commerce. Or perhaps you are to undergo some indeterminate period of punishment in which your sins are purged off and your character reformed by the flames of a great forge.

A resounding *no* to all the above!

Would you be very surprised to know that the One who created the heavens and the Earth, and saw that it was very good, is the same One who will personally take it upon Himself to transform you into a new creature who can stand next to the brightest angel and not be ashamed?

In the twinkling of an eye non other than the Lord Jesus Christ will remake you into a creature so wonderful that the very Creator of the Universe will stand next to you, his prized workmanship, and welcome you into His family.

If that does not take your very breath away and leave you staggering for an appropriate response, then you need to think about it until it does.

WHAT IS HEAVEN?

Christians are fond of asking non-Christians where they think they would go if they died that very day. Heaven or Hell? This is the ultimate question?

I am not implying that this isn't a good question. Our final destination is always worth considering. But I think before we ask this question we need to have a biblical concept of Heaven.

What is Heaven?

Almost 25 years ago I sat across from a prominent pastor and asked him what his thoughts were regarding Heaven.

I asked the question because after months of sitting under his preaching I began to have serious questions about the focus of his ministry.

The question was asked in a non-confrontational moment and elicited the following remarks.

"Heaven for me" he reported, "is a one room log cabin out in the middle of large green woods. I see a cook stove and a stone fireplace. I am sitting in a rocking chair cleaning my hunting gun and thinking about the crystal clear creek I will soon visit with my fly rod in hand."

"Is anyone with you?" I asked. The pastor leaned forward and smiled. "My hunting dog."

This may not be a word for word account, but it does capture the essence of the conversation.

I was stunned into silence as it sunk in that he was serious. After this encounter I determined to present my Christian friends with the same challenge.

"Describe heaven."

The responses were sobering to say the least. I listened

as my friends talked about pizza, basketball, endless tennis, fishing, canoeing, more fishing, food, hikes, picnics, long walks in the woods, hiking through the woods, strolling through fruit laden orchards and flying.

It soon occurred to me that the question, "describe heaven," for them meant "what would bring *me* the most pleasure".

Do you imagine, Christian, that your most treasured affections and deepest satisfactions can be met by fishing, pizza, long walks, picnics, food of every description, flying, and a thousand other delights and pleasures?

Is this what your soul longs for? Ask yourself what Heaven is and fill in the blanks. Be honest!

Jesus told his disciples that he would return for them so that where he was *they might be also*.

> Does your soul leap at the thought of communion with the Savior of your soul? Do you not desire above all else – and to the exclusion of every other thought that might now or ever enter your head – to be united in fellowship, in close proximity and forever bound with unbreakable cords of love and admiration to Jesus?

Not so sure? You are not alone.

Have you ever wondered if you are prepared to make the journey to Heaven?

It is my prayer that you continue reading this little book and reconsider your preferences and passions in light of God's revelation about Himself and the reality of Heaven.

The highest glory and greatest pleasure for a saint in Heaven is to be near to his God. There is no other preference that even comes close.

This exemplifies, summarizes, and reigns supremely above anything else that might now or ever be called *good*. It is the foremost and supplanting good from which all other forms of goodness are rooted.

> The foremost and ultimate good is to be near to God!

And close on its heels is the full exercise of all your new heavenly facilities in an endless and constant action, with all the powers of both body and soul, to seek but one thing. What is that one thing?

All the powers of our body and soul will be constantly exercised in the enjoyment of God!

So lets summarize what we have learned so far. The Everlasting Rest secured for the saints conforms to and pre-supposes five principles.

THE FIVE PRINCIPLES

1. **The first:** the means of grace come to an end.

2. **The second:** the rest reserved for the saints is free from all evil.

3. **The third:** the saint will undergo a personal perfecting in both body and soul.

4. **The fourth:** the foremost and ultimate good is to be near to God.

5. **And finally:** all the powers of our body and soul will be constantly exercised in the enjoyment of God.

Do these five designs fit into your concept of Heaven?

Perhaps this is all a little difficult to digest. All the more reason for you to explore the saint's everlasting rest.

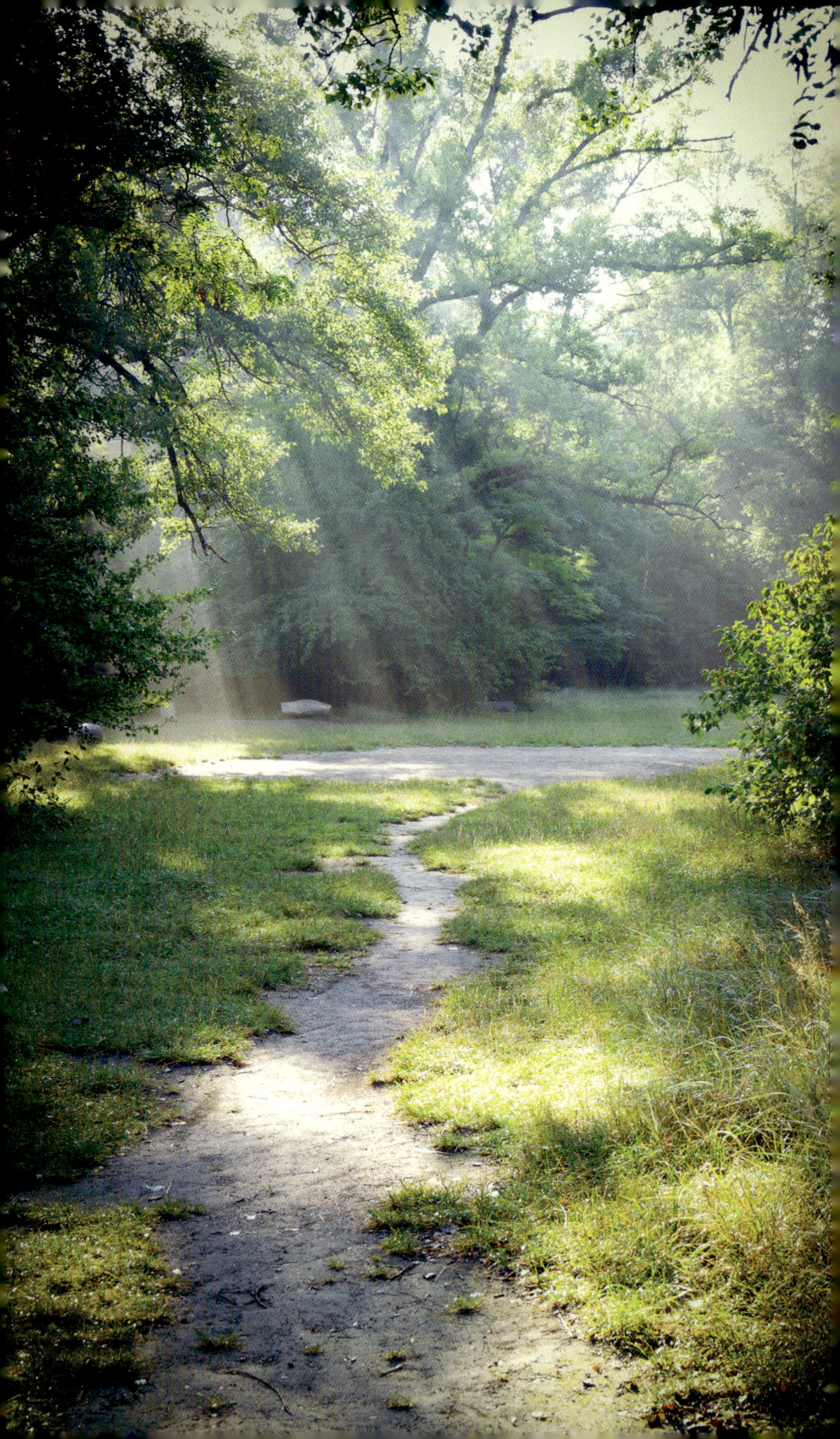

Chapter 3

Enjoyment of God
. . . and those who fear it

LET'S be honest and admit that we have difficulty when it comes to the idea of finding our greatest joy and enjoyment in God. Why?

The answer is found in the most tragic event of all Mankind. I am speaking now of Adam's fall and the resulting lost condition we now find ourselves in. And it affects us all!

Have you ever reflected on what was lost in that sad moment of history? Certainly our interest and enjoyment of God was lost. But is there more?

> Did we not lose all spiritual knowledge of our God and Creator? Did we not shift all our dispositions away from any hopes of joy and blessedness with God as its object? Is this not our natural condition as a result of our falling out with God?

In our fallen and lost condition – alone without some outside intervention – is there any hope of eternal happiness and glory?

Tragically the answer is a resounding *no*!

It is here that we find the dark nugget, the deep throbbing truth that is rooted in the diffidence and rebellion that ever exercises its death grip upon the heart, soul and imagination of Man. Here is the truth that casts a light on our withered souls.

Unregenerate Man – and it can be added many who profess to be Christians – cannot imagine enjoying God or finding any happiness in his presence. In fact the opposite is both feared and imagined.

If all joy has fled, all hope is gone, and not even the remnant of some little flickering light that illumines the goodness of God is present, then what is left?

The answer is seen over and over again in the sad history of the Israelites, who found it almost impossible to believe God had procured for them an earthly place of rest, let alone a heavenly one.

And when they did meditate on the coming Messiah it was always only to improve and bless their condition here on Earth.

And it was into this atmosphere that the Messiah did come. And when the Son of God disclosed His recovering grace and revealed that there was an eternal happiness and glory to be entered into by faith, he found no faith in Man to believe it.

And without faith our condition remains impossible and God remains displeased, justifying all our worst secret fears.

Doubt plays hard against disclosing and even harder against actually believing that Jesus Christ has procured a *rest* for those who put their trust in him. We want to substitute the promised rest with something more familiar and appealing to our senses.

> This is the common response of Man. Sadly it is also in itself a form of depravity and rebellion.

We find ourselves rehearsing the very question that Satan implanted into the mind of Eve. The question has a thousand forms but can best be summarized as follows:

> Does God really know what is best for me?

And let's be honest, does He really think I would be content to simply rest in His presence? Our ambitions, pride and affections war against the very thought of it.

Rest is something I tuck between my own great achievements. Surely something better awaits me than simply to rest?

And so we remain restless. It is at this juncture that we must ask the following questions:

What is it that is the sum of all the gospel promises?

What waits for us at the end of all life's challenges?

What is the compact sum of all the promises made to believers?

What is more welcome after a life of personal afflictions, tiring duties, disappointments and suffering?

What word sounds more soothing than any other after enduring tribulation for the sake of the Gospel?

Is there a greater reward for the vigor of our love for the Savior then entering into His rest?

What sustains us as we seek to honor our God in a world that is spending all its energies to misappropriate His glorious name and separate it from any connection to His creation?

What greater promise sustains us and gives us stability as we walk the King's narrow highway toward the Celestial City?

And finally, what greater privileges can a Christian have than to know – yes, to depend upon and give constant thought to – the *rest* that awaits him?

THE ANXIETY OF A RESTLESS SPIRIT

Are you caught up in the cares and concerns of this world? Are you anxious over much?

Is your restless spirit ever seeking new ways to find peace, and always disappointed upon reaching the milestones set up by this world?

I beg you to consider the everlasting and unchanging state of *rest* that awaits those who take God in Christ for their only rest and affix their very essence of heart and soul upon Him and no other.

May the living God, who is the author of the only rest that can satisfy the deep and abiding longings of your soul, grant you a spiritual mind and a heavenly heart so that you might secure your rest in Him.

> What is it that prevents you, Christian, from making the act of loving of Him who bought you, and the delighting in Him who redeemed you, the work of your life?
>
> I can tell you what it is with some certainty. It is either unbelief or negligence.
>
> And what will be the consequences of these twin sins? You will come short of it.

You risk missing the promise by being turned out of

the path of life, and never entering into *His rest.*

Let me make a provocative pronouncement that is based on Gods revelation: *The most happiness that can ever be attained is found in the rest promised by our Lord.*

It is by way of description the perfect and endless enjoyment of God by those saints that have been perfected by God.

Now, please consider the brief illustration in the next chapter.

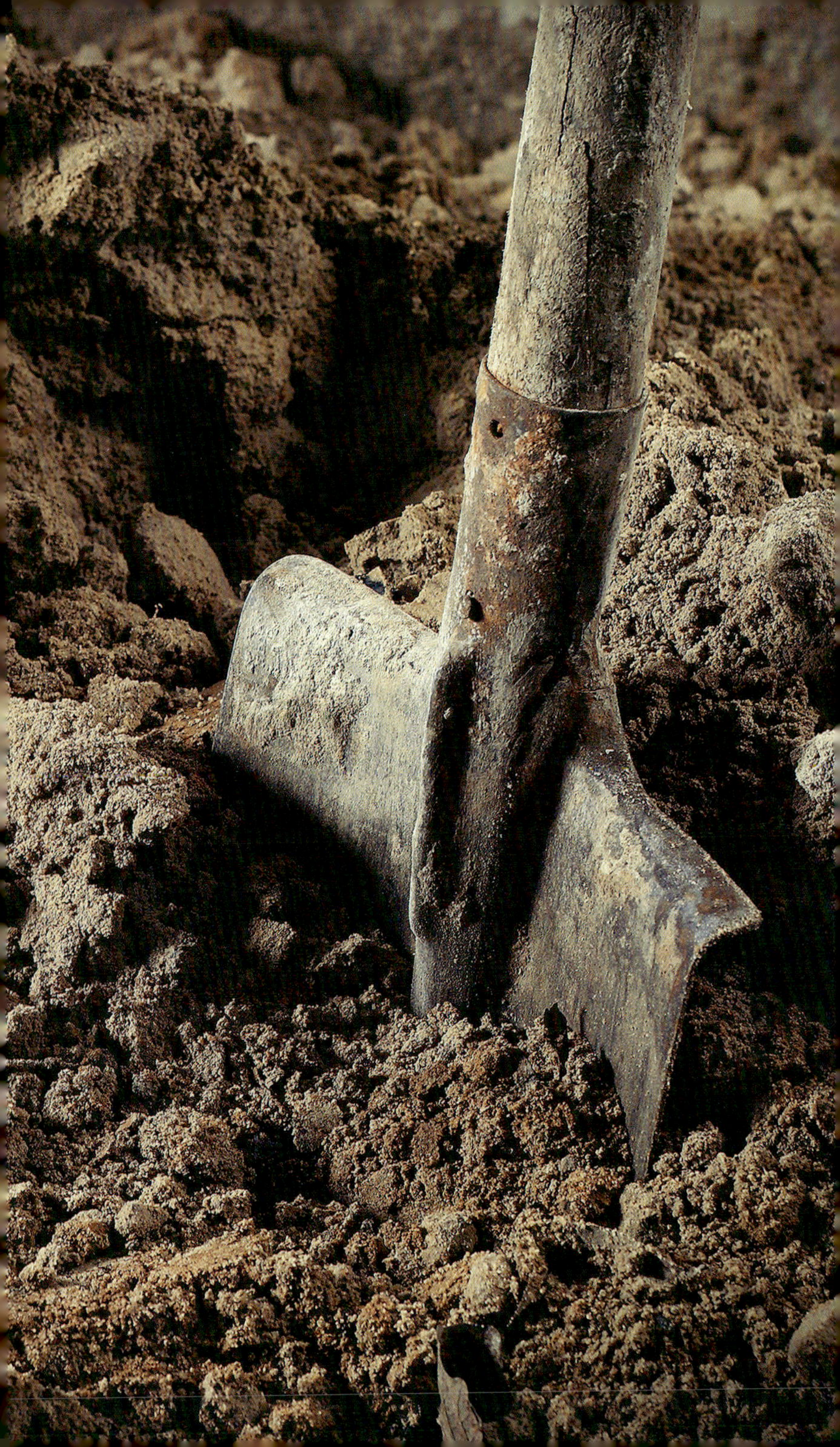

Chapter 4

Digging holes

... a parable

A great king and his entourage arrived in a far country. They carried with them hundreds of shovels. The king sent out his servants to invite the citizens of this country to a meeting set on a certain day and hour.

When the meeting time arrived more than half the population of the town came to find out what it was all about.

The king took the stage and made this simple announcement, "I am going away to collect a great treasure. And when I return it is my desire to give it freely to the citizens of this country."

There was a gasp followed by applause. The king held up his hand to quiet the crowd and continued, "I have brought with me these shovels which you may pick up after the conclusion of this meeting. It will be your task to dig a hole in a prominent place on your property. When I return I will fill each man's hole up to the very top with treasure."

Then one day it happened. The great king was seen returning to the town with tens of thousands of his soldiers and an endless train of wagons all heaped up with treasure.

True to his word the great king commanded his troops to pour his treasure into the holes that had been dug by those few who believed the promise and invested hard work into the promise he had made so many years ago.

THE UNDERLYING LESSON

Now let me put the finishing touch on the truth that undergirds this very poor illustration.

The most happiness that can ever be attained is found in the rest promised by our Lord. It is by way of description the perfect and endless enjoyment of God by those saints who have been perfected by God. And the enjoyment they receive will be according to the measure of their capacity that is arrived at by their souls upon their death.

An enjoyment to be realized fully after the resurrection of the dead and the final judgment. Put another way: Heaven will *not be the same* for all saints.

And what is the lesson, and how should it impact you?

The answer: Invest in the promise! Prepare for Heaven now!

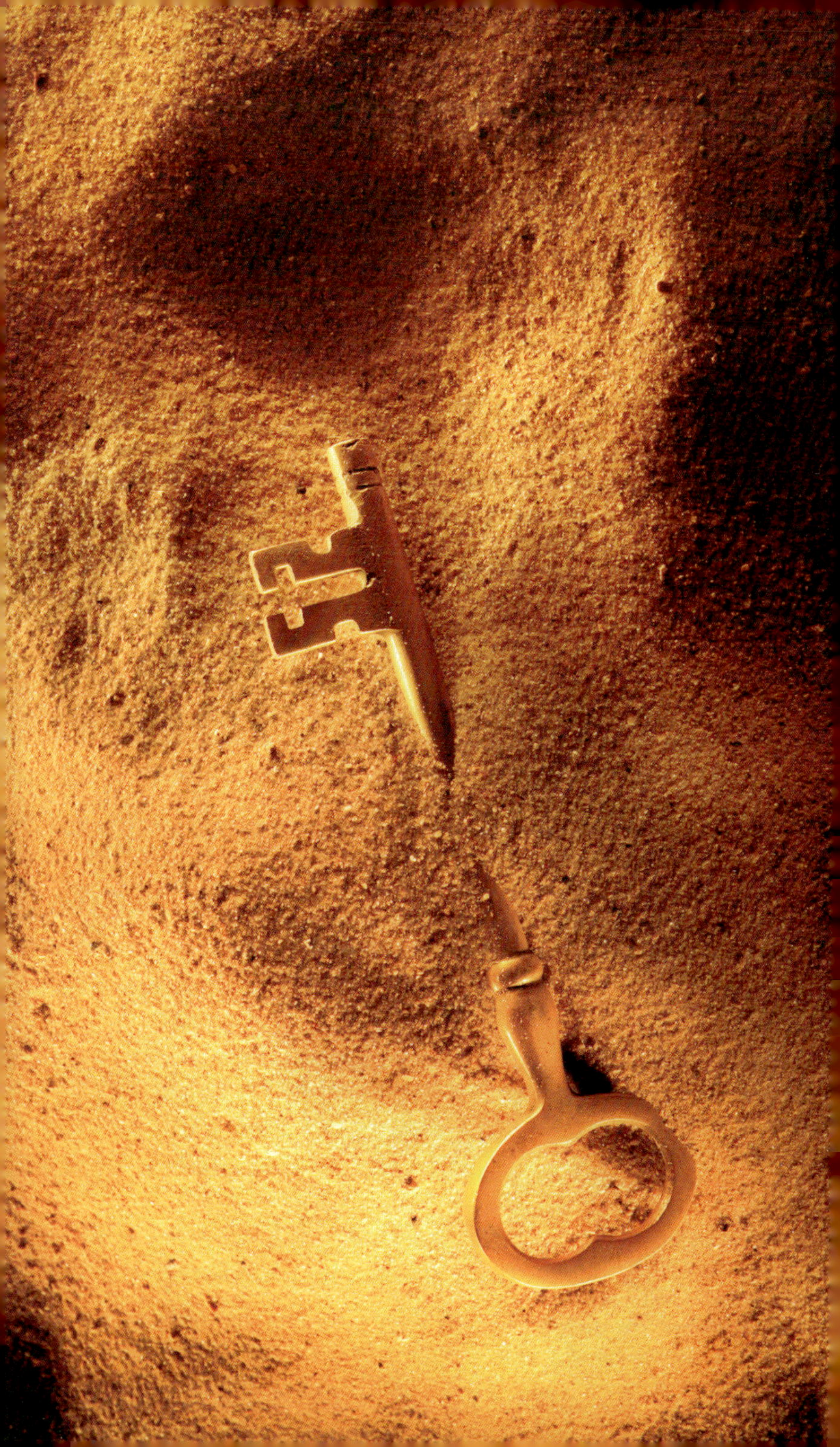

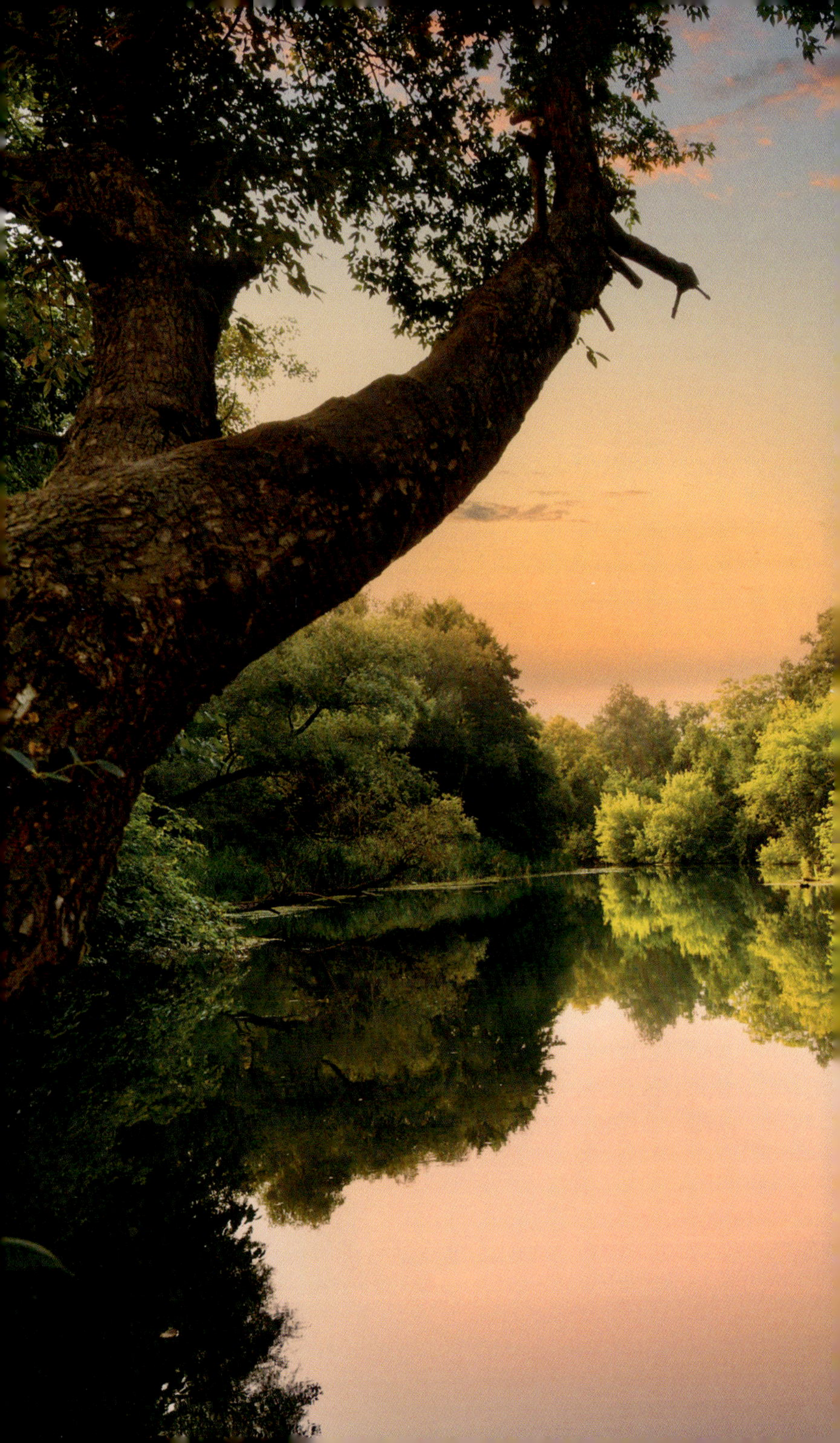

Chapter 5

The nature of Rest
. . . and the foundation of the promise

BEFORE we further advance the necessity of preparing for the saint's everlasting rest, let us explore what is presupposed in the nature of this rest.

Obviously it is mortal men who are to seek it, not angels or glorified spirits who already have it. No devils seek this rest nor should they.

Also, it is only for those put their trust in Jesus Christ and place their destiny in His hands. It is they who may expect that in this glorious surrender all happiness and joy will be ultimately guaranteed.

Conversely, placing confidence in anyone or anything other than God's Son disqualifies and annuls the promise of rest.

It must also be stated clearly that Mankind is a far distance from the promise of eternal rest. This is the woeful case of Mankind since The Fall.

When Christ comes with regenerating grace, does he find Man sitting still in anticipation of the great gift? *No.*

Instead Christ finds men running with all their might toward certain eternal ruin.

Mankind is making haste toward Hell at such a pace that the claims of Christ appear as a blur seen out of the corner of the eye. Our focus is more often fixed upon the mad rush of humanity sprinting down the broad highway that leads to death.

It is only a Holy Spirit inspired heart failure that brings men to a standstill, gasping under the conviction of sin and Hell.

It is only then that by the miracle of regenerative conversion that men receive new hearts that are attracted to and attuned to live sincerely for the Savior.

It is at the point of conversion that both the distance from and the true knowledge of this distance from the promise of eternal rest are revealed.

The vast majority of this world does not know that they are without God. They do not have a clue that they are on the way to Hell. And they certainly do not know the way to Heaven.

And here is the proof of it:

Can a man know that he has lost his soul and the God that created it and not cry out in anguish, "I am unraveled?"

Can a man truly know that he is dangling over the fires of Hell by the thin fragile cord of time and not cry out with urgency, "Please save me?"

Do not be amazed that few men obtain the everlasting rest so freely offered by the Savior – as few men are convinced that there is such a rest.

It is not that they think themselves a distance from it but that *they do not think of it at all.*

You will not seek to find something that you do not know is lost to you.

You will not seek a remedy for an illness you do not think you have. And isn't that exactly what the Lord predicted.

> Mark 2:17
> When Jesus heard it, he saith unto them, They that are whole have no need of the physician, but they that are sick: I came not to call the righteous, but sinners to repentance.

The distance we find ourselves from the promised rest is not only revealed to us by God, but it is then God Himself that moves us toward our rest.

Baxter calls this the influence of a superior moving cause. "And without it we would all stand still, not moving any longer toward the precipice, but neither moving toward the promised rest."

How very important and instructive it is for us to reach and understand this moment of fearful paralysis. It is like the recurring dream in which the fire, flood or foe is descending upon you and you cannot move.

Your mind wishes to move, but you are paralyzed and absolutely helpless. Yes that describes it very well. Helpless!

You are now ready to grasp and hold on tight to the most fundamental wisdom of the Christian faith. The foundational truth that constantly is proving itself in our pilgrimage up the King's highway.

The great center point of all our thoughts about God and his Christ should be echoing in our ears as we hear it from the very mouth of God.

> John 15:5
> I am the vine, ye are the branches: He that abideth in me, and I in him, the same bringeth forth much fruit: for without me ye can do nothing.

There it is! What is the foundation of the promised *rest*? To be *with God*. And if he is absent? You can do *nothing*!

Memorize it! Two words – *Without Me*! What is our prayer but that the Lord will remember us when he comes into His kingdom?

Jesus was not the only one hanging on a cross at Calvary. There was another, a man who represented you and me. He was a thief and a robber. He had a message for all sinners that he uttered that day, a woeful cry laced with but a pittance of hope. It was he who cried, "Remember me."

Our last words should be filled with great reservoirs of hope deposited over a lifetime of communion with the Savior.

Remember His great promises to those who put their trust in Him and you to can joyfully utter these final words, "Remember Me."

And what is the reply to those who trust the Savior? Is it not the only promise that undergirds your entire existence and gives it hopeful meaning?

Can you not now even hear it ring like a freedom bell? Jesus promises that you will be with Him.

Is this not *rest*?

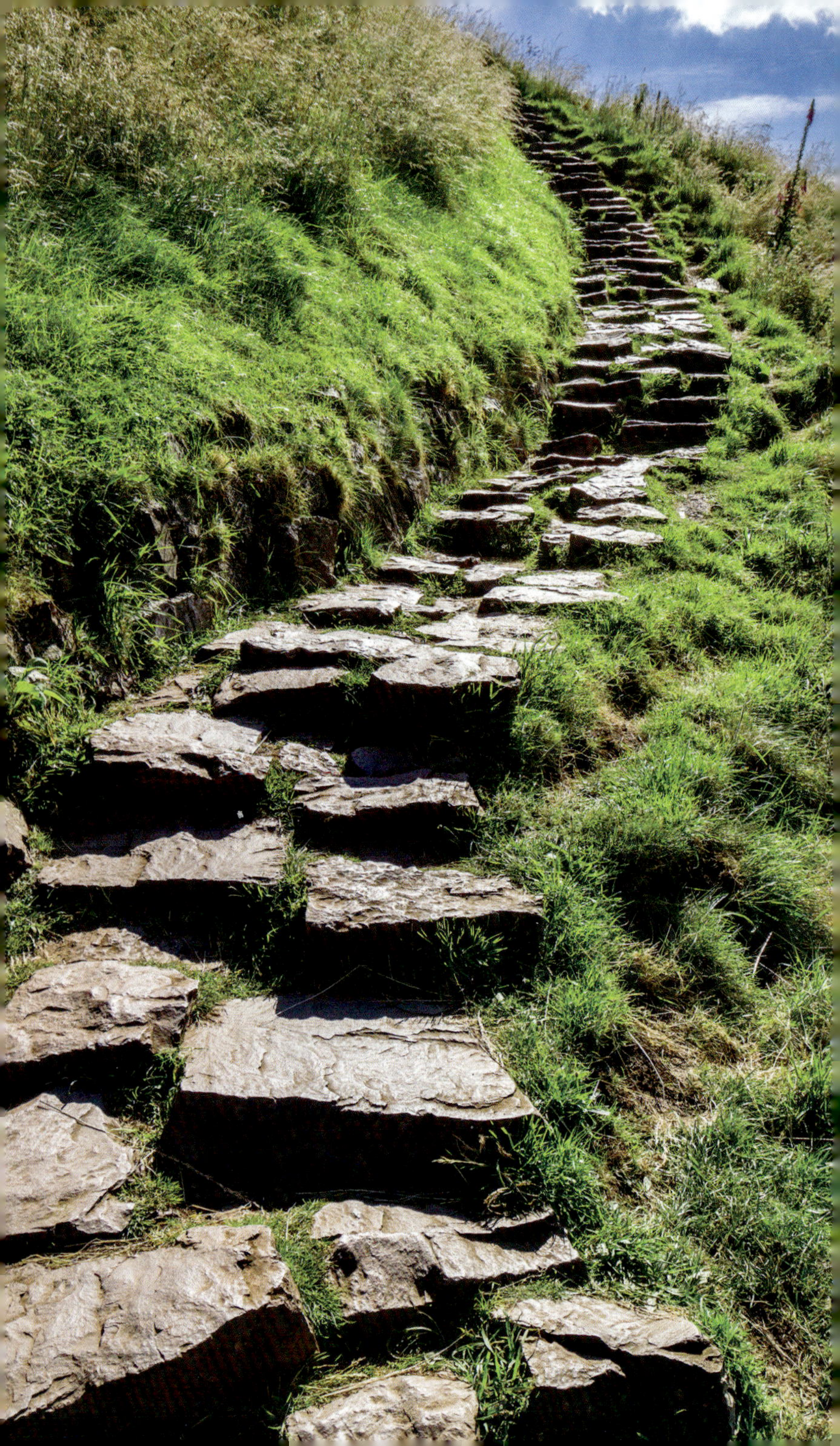

Chapter 6

With *Me* or without Me!

And the paradox of burden

IS there a corresponding consequential truth that quakes the withered soul and sends the crippled heart into a tornado of fear?

Is it not the dreaded words – *"Depart from me"* – spoken by the Lord Himself? This followed by a full revelation of the simple truth that "Without me you can do nothing."

We are all, every one of us, subject to the strict conditions of one of two promises from the Creator. And the results have been forecast in a hundred messages directly from the Creator.

The ultimate and only meaningful consequence of all of this life is that you will either end up being "in" or "outside" the presence of the Lord Jesus Christ. You will be *with* Christ or you will be *without* Christ!

"With me." Were more comforting words ever spoken? But, you might protest, that was for the thief. And I reply – yes, and for you also if you would cast yourself upon His mercy and seek His face bloodied and scarred and see with new eyes that you have a Savior in Jesus.

And for a moment – rather than cast your mind on all the benefits of knowing and living in the presence of your Creator – simply imagine the opposite.

Imagine all the emptiness and hopelessness contained in the world. Now imagine the most joyless and friendless confinement your mind can muster.

Add fear, loathing, reprisal, recrimination and brutality of every sort. Now pour in vast quantities of bitterness and hatred and mix it all together into a boiling, fuming, swirling black hole from which there is no escape.

Finally see the brew's fumes ignited by a great fire that burns eternally and is never extinguished. Now add yourself to this fiery cauldron and you begin to have an inkling of what it will be like to be *without* the Lord Jesus Christ.

Your life really does ultimately settle down to two simple choices. They are to be with Jesus Christ or without Him. His sufficiency or your utter lack of it. Dependence upon Him or to be ever without him.

"Will you be with me," Jesus asks. "Or will you be without me. Will I know you or will you depart from me forever a stranger? Your everlasting rest is in the balance."

Does this add some urgency to this question: How do I find this rest?

> "Those that seek this rest have an inward principle of spiritual life. God does not move men like stones, but he endows them with life, not to enable them to move without Him, but in subordination to Himself, the first mover." – Richard Baxter

How can you find this rest? On your own you will not and cannot. You are unwilling and unable to move into God's perfect rest. And this is wonderful news because it secures our souls to an immovable truth.

Look to the skies, do you see that eagle effortlessly lifted into the sky by the warm invisible draft of buoyant air?

Look to the river and observe the leaves carried off the riverbank and into the current that moves them effortlessly to the seashore.

The eagle is not master of the skies. He is the willing servant of its silent ever-moving pathways. He was made for the sky and the sky was made to accommodate every intricacy of his splendid design. And who made and choreographed all this? Was it not the Lord

Jesus Christ?

The eagle – endowed with life and enabled by inward principles which it did not learn or construct – soars majestically in the heavens. And so it is with us who have been graced by the Savior.

The Lord does not wrench us up and drag us to his rest. No, he awakens us to His plans. He enables us by His very Spirit and He beckons us to come to Him, to seek Him, to rest in Him. And if we have been so endowed with this principle of spiritual life we will seek and find our *rest* in Him.

So not only does this seeking after the promised rest presuppose an inward principle of spiritual life, it also supposes that the result of this principle is the continual movement of the soul in earnest labor toward the everlasting rest.

Jesus calls this the light burden carried by those who follow Him. This is not to say that the path through this life is going to be easy for the follower of Jesus.

We are promised quite the opposite. But His burden is light. Can we begin to understand this paradox? The answer is found in the *way* to the destination of *rest*.

Let us explore further . . .

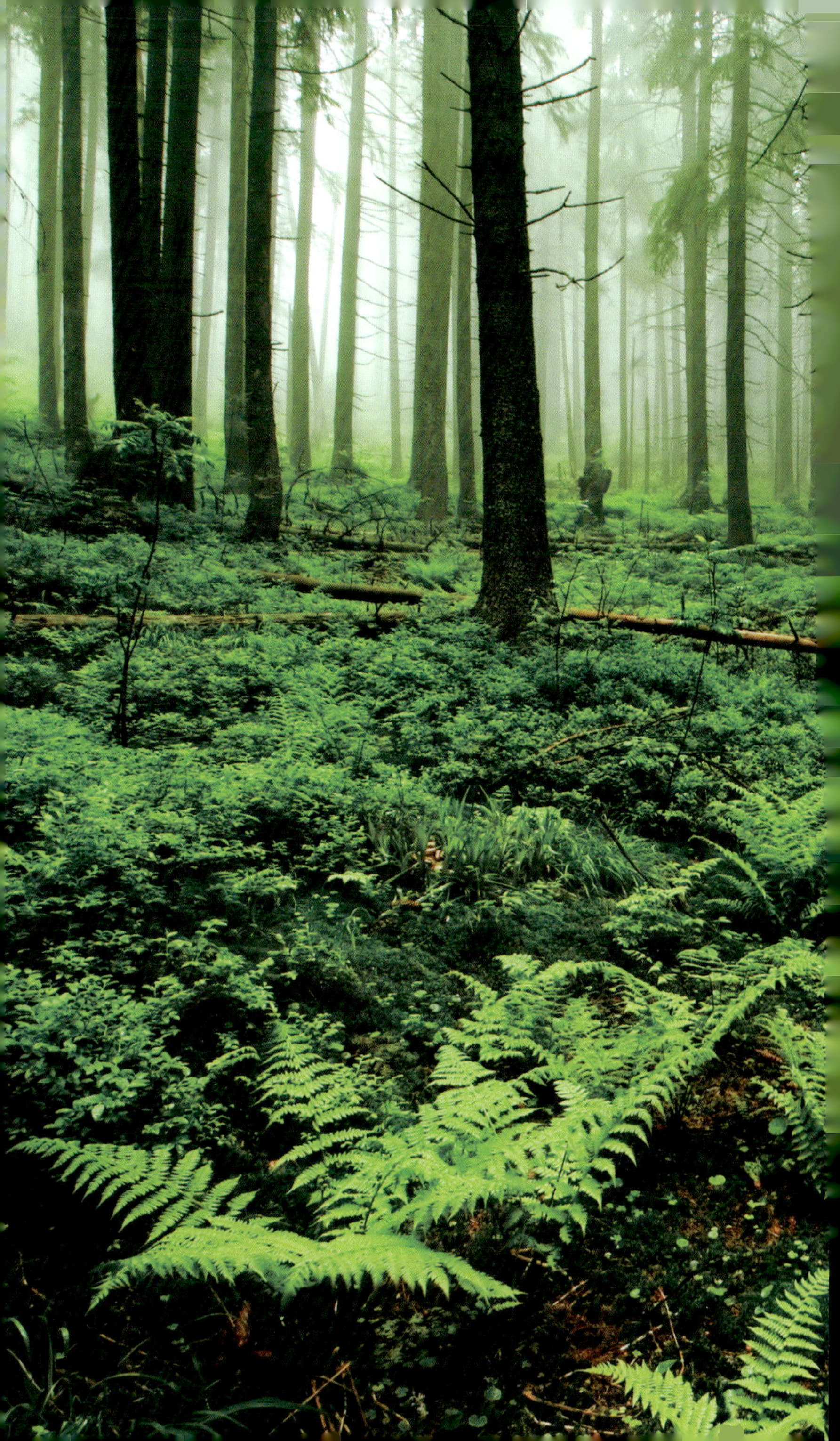

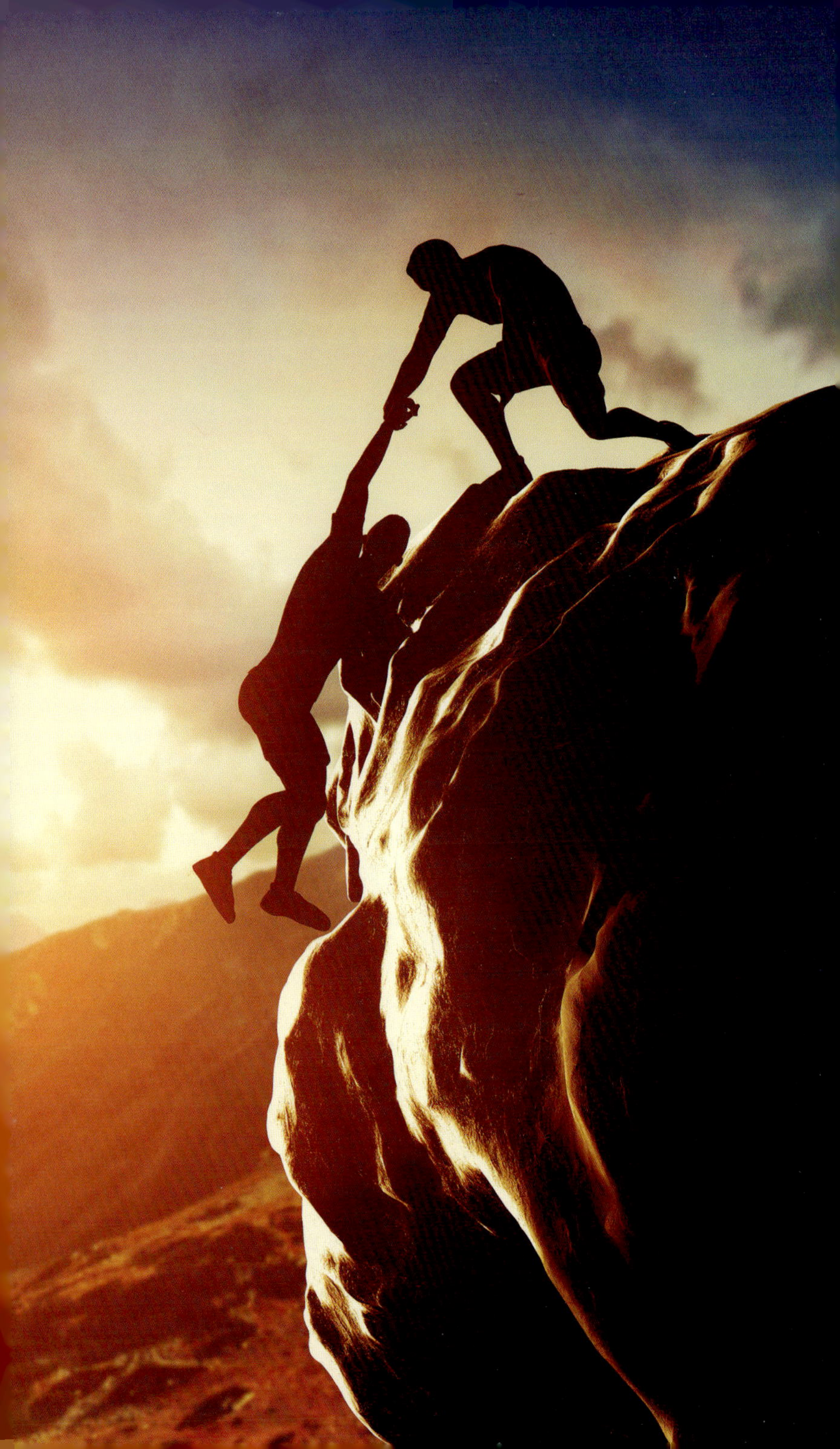

Chapter 7

The difficult path that leads to Rest

...and what must be left behind

OUR only pathway to rest is through the Lord Jesus Christ, and so the Savior calls himself the *door*. We are told that few enter through this door. It leads to a narrow way that few seek.

Though it may seem a paradox, do not stumble at the paramount truth that the kingdom of Heaven is entered by violence.

The picture could not be clearer. It is a door few enter that leads to a narrow path that even fewer seek. Once entered it promises struggles so severe that the only way to describe them is with military language.

But Why? Why does the Lord make it difficult to enter the narrow gate – so difficult that many desire to enter but few actually do? And only those who endure to the end secure the promise given to those who would follow Christ.

for the Lord who has saved them and is calling them to find their everlasting rest in Him, and Him alone.

Is there a better way to accomplish this than to make the journey a struggle designed to constantly remind us of His sufficiency and discourage us from grasping for or hoping in anything else?

God can do very nicely without our love. But His love for us – something expressed out of His very essence – produces a mercy that is for *our* benefit, not His.

And so it is for us that He is jealous. It is for our welfare that He forbids any other so called gods. It is so that our enjoyment will be pure and without defect that he insists that *He alone* be the object of our affection.

The modern concept that God needs our fellowship is incorrect. That God desires our fellowship is a sweet mystery that has nothing to do with neediness and everything to do with the immeasurable love of God.

What is very clear is that we desperately need Him.

He is our everlasting rest!

Now we can end this book with a glancing review from a different perspective of the five things contained in the saint's heavenly rest.

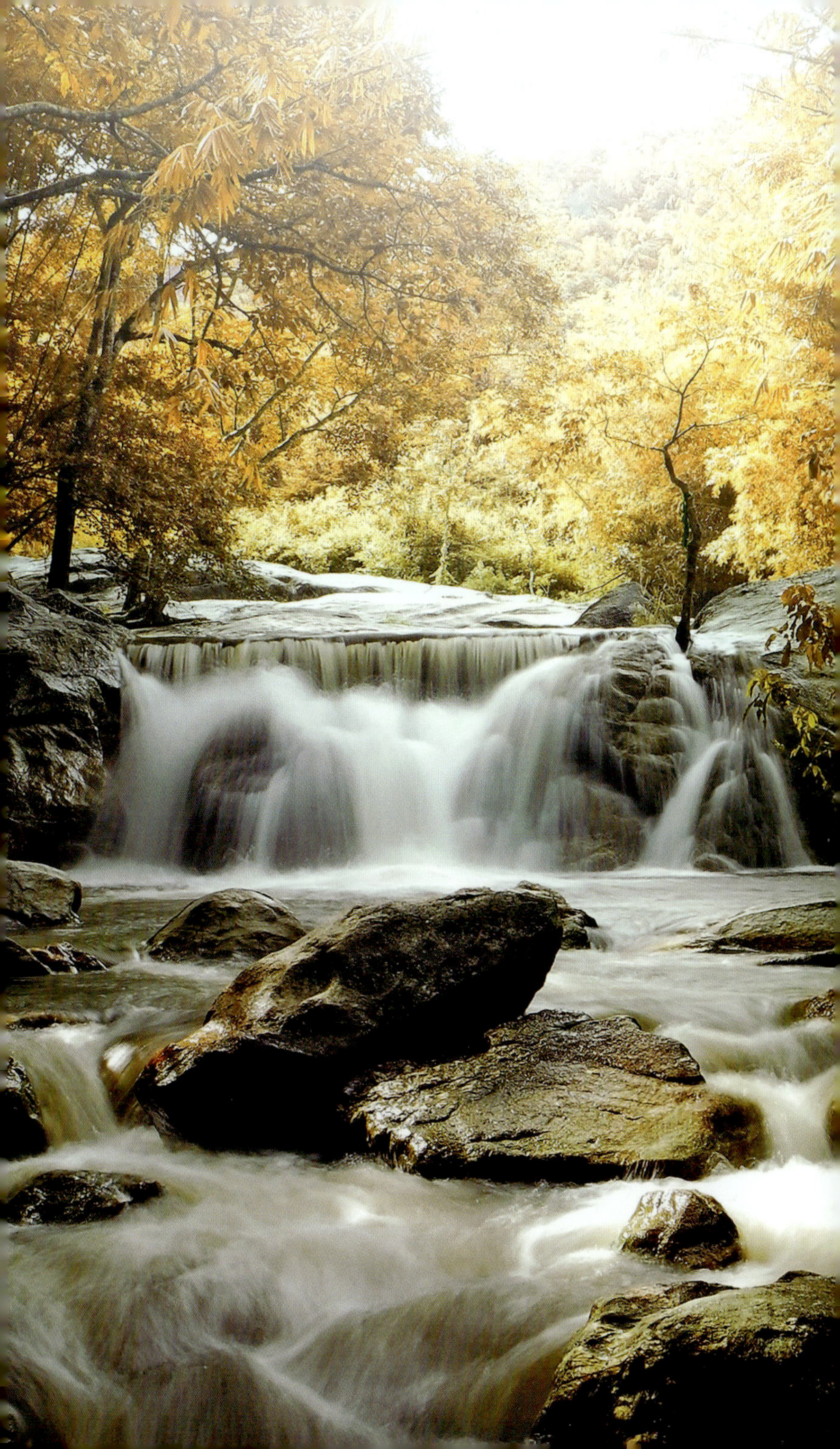

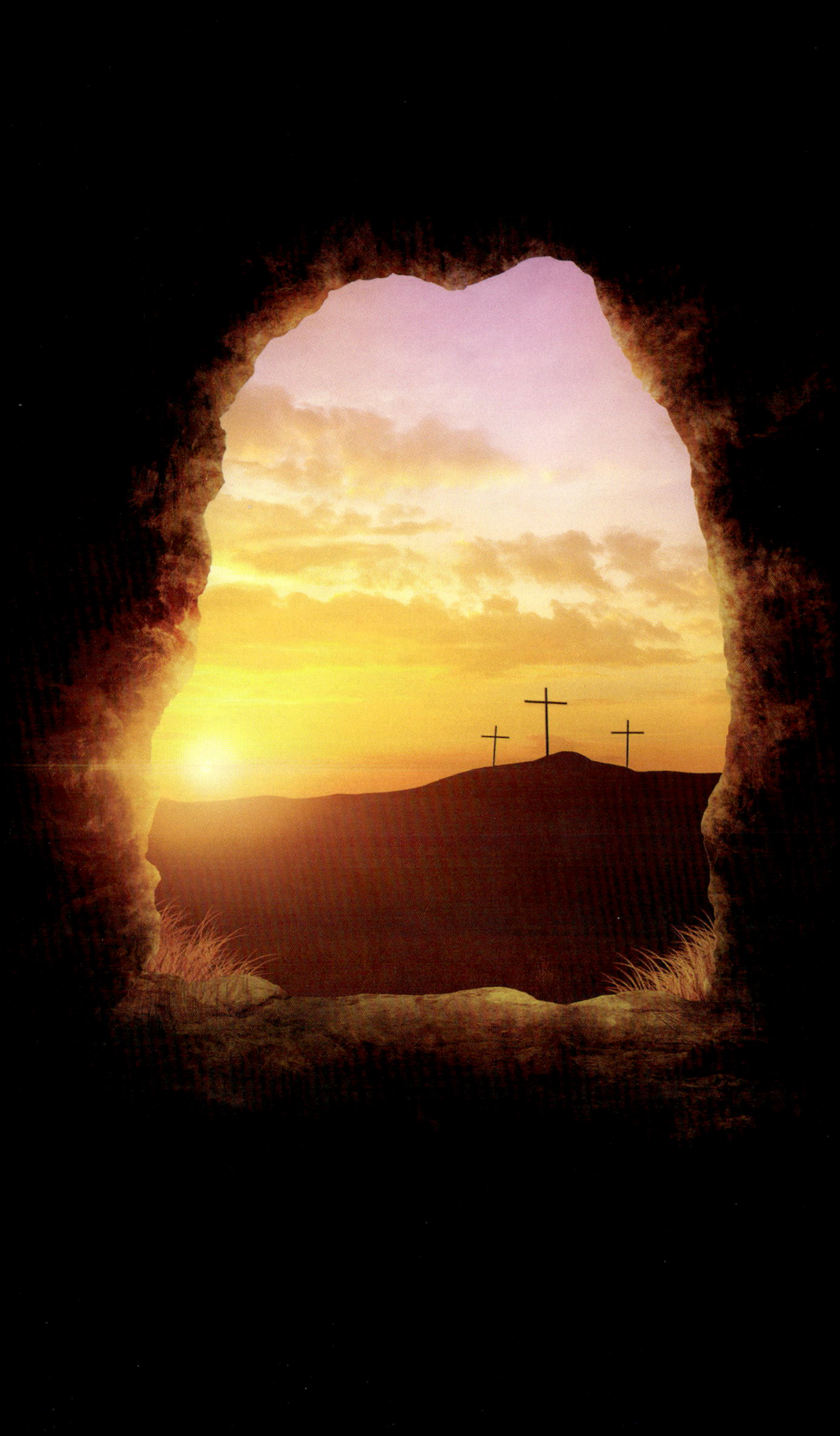

Chapter 8

When evil can no longer torment or threaten you

WHEN a ship has finished its voyage and enters the still waters of the harbor, the means necessary for safe arrival cease.

When a carpenter receives his final payment for building a house it is because his work is finished.

When the full enjoyment of everything you have prayed earnestly for under the direction of the Holy Spirit comes to pass, a prayer is no longer needed.

Preaching the gospel and the other ministries of Man will come to an end. No need to fast since the gulf between good and evil is fixed for eternity and evil can no longer torment or threaten you. The unregenerate are beyond any hope and the saints are beyond any fear.

There is a ceasing of the means of grace.

All the evils that accompanied us through the course of our entire life are banished from our presence. All the obstacles that made us stumble have been removed.

And so it must be, for in Heaven there is nothing that is unclean or defiling. All that is not the perfect good is left outside – forever past our view in the utter darkness that we may never enter.

Also left behind is all sorrow and grief. There is no place in heaven for feeble bodies, painful infirmities, sickness of any kind, consuming cares or the grip of fear.

When the world rejoiced we wept, and now our sorrow is turned to everlasting joy that can never be taken from us.

There is an everlasting rest that is free from all evil.

No matter how great the glory, how bright the lights, how glad the music, they mean nothing to the deaf and blind. But as it is written . . .

> 1 Corinthians 2:9
> Eye hath not seen, nor ear heard, neither have entered into the heart of man, the things which God hath prepared for them that love him.

Our mortal eyes and ears cannot comprehend, nor are they capable of seeing or hearing the wonders that Gods has prepared for His saints.

This truth should give us great hope and anticipation. This truth, by inference, discloses something that we should find wondrous: *There is nothing on Earth to compare to what awaits us in Heaven.*

We have never experienced anything like what now is being prepared for us – ready when the time comes for us to enter His everlasting rest.

This should brighten the soul and cause the imagination to leap with anticipation.

Something so good that your present experience in this world gives you no perspective upon which to judge it.

It is utterly and completely unique and inscrutable to our current senses.

> The keener your eyesight, the more glorious the sunset.
>
> The finer your hearing, the sweeter the symphony.
>
> And so it follows that the more perfected the soul, the more glorious and joyous the splendors prepared for the saints as they enter their everlasting rest.

The saint is prepared for the everlasting rest by the personal perfection of body and soul.

And though it is almost impossible to convey without fearing that my words devalue the truth, I will try my best to give expression to the truth: That it is the nearness to – our *proximity* to God – that is the chief good.

The simple truth is that we know very little about what it is to know God. And if I know so little, how can I imagine the enjoyment of Him? I know next to nothing about spirits. How then can I apprehend the essence of the Father of Spirits?

I have the true reflection of God in His Son Jesus Christ. And I can learn of Him and thus know something of God. But given my human limitation, even that lifelong investigation leaves me standing before an ocean with but a teaspoon to draw out its treasures.

Jesus promised us that when he appeared we would be like Him, and to behold Him as He is. So obviously, there is much to learn which we cannot now know. We must be patient and not leap too far ahead, or speculate about things for which we have little evidence to support.

The glass that stands between the creator and us darkens all our current apprehensions. And that is for our good. A glimpse is all we need for now.

But that should never keep us from joyfully anticipating by faith, knowing that God is always good to His word. And we are given a down payment on this truth in our spirits as we contemplate Christ. Isn't that what the scriptures teach? But as it is written:

1 Corinthians 2:9-10
Eye hath not seen, nor ear heard, neither have entered into the heart of man, the things which God hath prepared for them that love him.
But God hath revealed them unto us by his Spirit: for the Spirit searcheth all things, yea, the deep things of God.

The foremost and ultimate good is to be near to God.

How many examples in God's good creation do we have of creatures that are fit for a specific purpose?

Remove the purpose and the reason for the creature's being is forfeited. Remove the creature and the purpose for its existence is no longer realized. There is a mysterious design in all of creation. A symphony of actions and reactions produced and directed by a God with infinite skill.

Man in his great arrogance and lack of appreciation for the "very good" work our Lord has accomplished, seeks to improve on the Master's creation.

Like a child putting finishing touches on the Mona Lisa with a black crayon, Man enters the workshop of creation and begins to meddle. And what will be the result of this intrusion? Utter calamity!

Now do not mistake my meaning, as God gave Man a

garden and encouraged – no, *commanded* him – to tend it and manicure it for God's glory and Mans good.

I am not talking about the tilling of a field or the development of something useful by fashioning what God has placed at our disposal.

What I am talking about is altering the very creation of God – crossing the bright yellow line into areas reserved for and by the Creator only.

And what does Man do to prepare himself for eternity? Most do absolutely nothing. Others imagine that by some alteration he can make himself fit for the holy place – perhaps a tweak of the spiritual DNA will produce a result that is needed. The result, like Man's meddling with Gods good creation, will be the same. Calamitous!

As has already been mentioned, we are unfit for Heaven. Heaven is unfit for us, and we for it. That is the unalterable fact apart from the creative work of God.

Man can produce no such work that would ever make him fit for heaven. But God can.

Flesh and Blood cannot inherit the Kingdom of God, but a spiritual body may. And it just such a body that God will fashion for those who will enter his rest.

Whoever you are, if you are a child of God you will be

changed one day into a creature who, if you saw before you, would have you on your knees worshiping.

And like the angels, your new self would say, "Arise my dear friend. I am but a creature who was sown a perishable seed and by the good pleasure of God has been fashioned into a creature now fit for Heaven. "

Much could be speculated upon regarding this topic. A few things are revealed, and all of them ravish the soul and challenge the imagination. There is no need to go beyond what God has revealed:

1. Our current body is unfit for heaven.
2. We will be given a new body that is fashioned just for heaven, our place of everlasting rest.
3. This body will be more "real" than the body we now have. The bible tells us that the appearance of this body is not now presently knowable.
4. The new body though not yet knowable is "like" the body of the risen Lord Jesus Christ.
5. When fashioned with this new body we will see Jesus as He is.

After the Resurrection, the early disciples saw with human eyes the risen Lord Jesus Christ. A few things about that body have been revealed to us. It was inter-dimensional. He was capable of locating Himself without regard for walls or locked doors.

We can joyfully wonder with anticipation knowing that

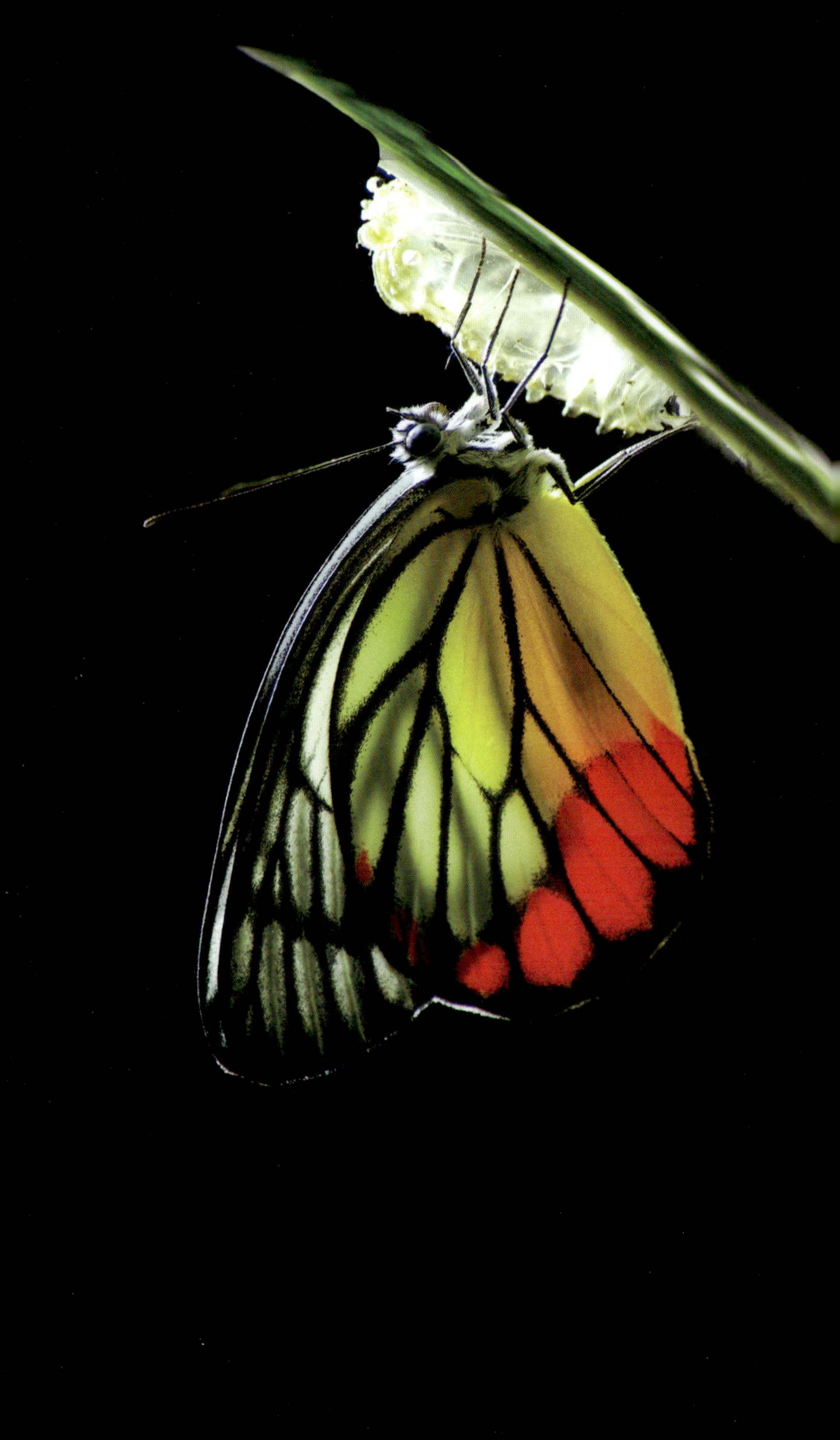

God always keeps His word and accomplishes His purpose. And if it is His good purpose for us to abide with Him forever, then we can be sure that it will be with a body and soul that is designed with all its newly created capacities and longings to find constant and unending enjoyment in God.

Gone the frail, diseased bodies of the flesh. Gone the thimble-sized senses – now enlarged to ocean capacity, filled up and brimming over with the happiness that can only come from He Himself.

It will be a blessed employment in a glorified body! To stand before the throne of God and the Lamb, and to shout with ever increasing unction:

> Revelation 5: 9-12
> And they sung a new song, saying, Thou art worthy to take the book, and to open the seals thereof: for thou wast slain, and hast redeemed us to God by thy blood out of every kindred, and tongue, and people, and nation;
>
> And hast made us unto our God kings and priests: and we shall reign on the earth.
>
> And I beheld, and I heard the voice of many angels round about the throne and the beasts and the elders: and the number of them was ten thousand times ten thousand, and thousands of thousands; Saying with a loud voice, Worthy is the Lamb that

was slain to receive power, and riches, and wisdom, and strength, and honour, and glory, and blessing.

Christians, *this* is the blessed rest – a rest, as it were, without rest – for "they rest not day and night, saying, Holy, holy, holy Lord God Almighty, who was, and is, and is to come."

And if this is how the body is employed in Heaven, what will our souls be about – our souls with powers and capacities greater than our bodies? The actions of our souls will be the mightiest and its enjoyments the sweetest.

The bodily senses have their proper function, and with those capacities unique to the body we receive and enjoy those things that are given to the body.

The soul has its own activity by which it moves.

> ". . . knowing and remembering, loving and delighting in the joy that can only we found in the Lord of Heaven. Our souls will be fit with heavenly eyes to see and heavenly arms to embrace the joys now set before it." – *Richard Baxter*

And consider this, my Christian friend: Knowledge of itself is a very desirable thing.

We know this is true in our present condition. Discovering the secrets of God's nature and the mysteries of

God's creation exceed most other delights.

Man delights to measure the Earth and the sun and moon and stars, and to forecast the next eclipse to the minute, years before it occurs. You can add a thousand other delights that are opened up to us by knowledge.

But one thing eludes us, and it is the most important knowledge of all. And this is the knowledge that will be the crown of all those who enter the saint's everlasting rest.

The most excellent knowledge is to know God, who is infinite and made all the other things about which you are so curious.

The saints will discover knowledge of God that will continue to unfold forever. You will be delighted beyond words with every new disclosure, and so it will always be.

There will never be a moment, if such a thing actually exists in Heaven, when you say, "Ah, now I have complete and full knowledge of my creator."

It will never happen.

Think about it for a moment. Not only will you never become weary of declaring the glory of God with increasing intensity and joy, but the glory you declare will be infused with new insights at an ever increasing and never decreasing pace – forever and ever.

The manna *from* Heaven will become the manna *in* Heaven, fresh every day and ever more succulent with each bite.

In the natural realm God has created in us an inclination to seek out truth. In the heavenly realm God will give us an inclination to seek out the ultimate infinite truth.

Whatever satisfaction is received in the exploration of truth incidental to God's creative masterpiece, it will be nothing compared to the dazzling wonder that is our heritage in Heaven.

The soul that rests in Christ will ultimately be the soul that rests forever in a Heaven that will never cease to astonish.

What was for the Apostle Paul unutterable will become the very atmosphere that surrounds and encompasses us with a blessed never-ending unstoppable impulse to gaze and praise.

The supreme excellence, which cannot be superseded by anything else, is to have our God as the object of all our affections, hopes and aspirations when we are armed with a perfect peace and total lack of apprehension.

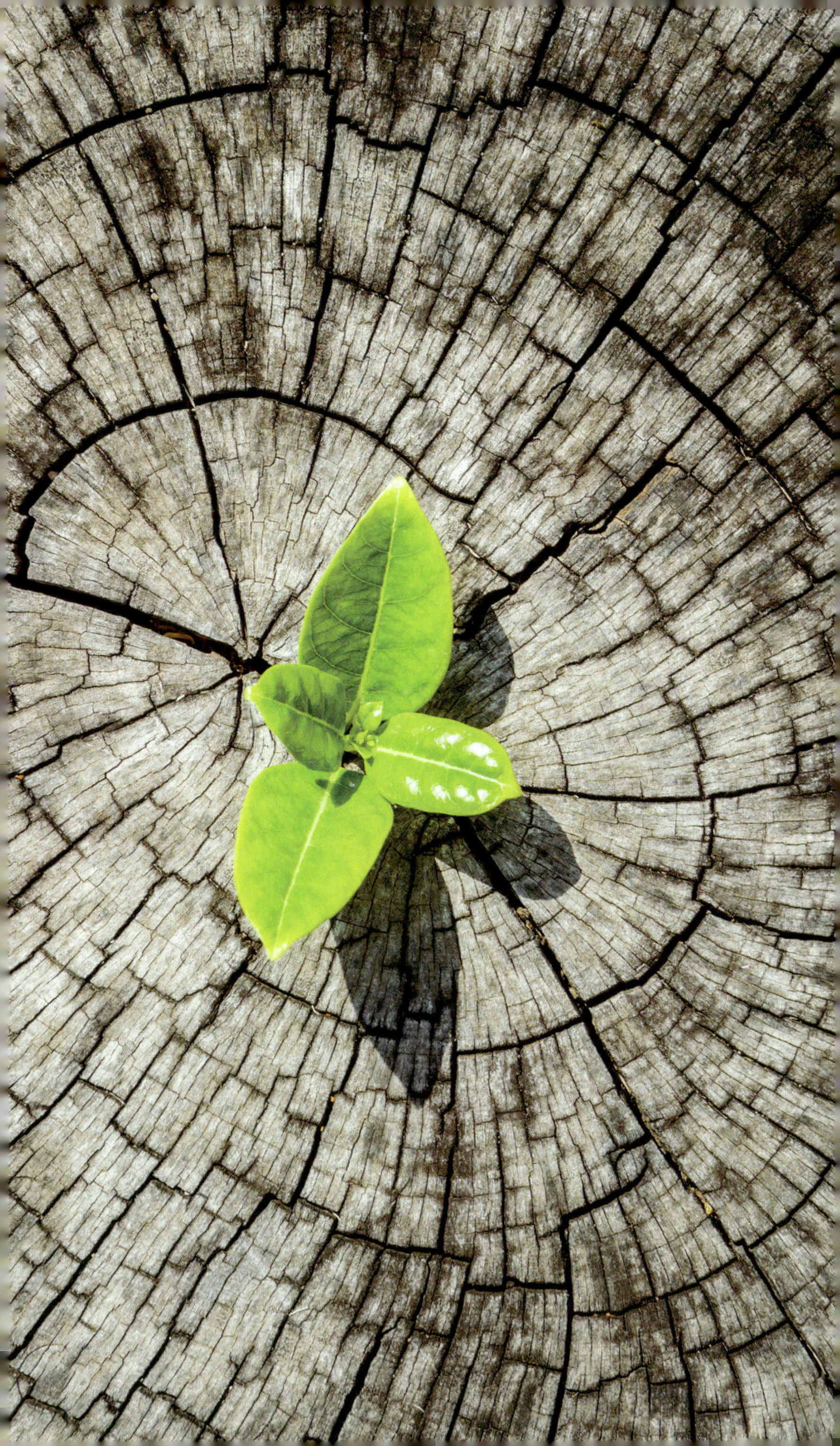

Free from the bondage of sin, we are at liberty to both approach and adore our Lord and Savior with true wisdom and understanding.

Didn't Peter give us a glimpse of this while on the mount of transfiguration? *"Master, it is good to be here."*

But gone will be the terror, replaced by perfect peace and endless delight. There will be no coming down off the mountain. The words of the Savior saying, "tell no man what you have seen" will be replaced by an endless telling of not only what has been seen, but what is being seen.

Imagine your best! Twist up your mind into a ready state of ecstasy and let all the praise for your Lord lift up your soul to Heaven.

Do this and a thousand other things to raise yourself up and you will have accomplished *nothing* when compared to the reality of the saint's everlasting rest.

We cannot imagine the unimaginable. But we can taste it, glimpse it as Moses did while hidden by God in the cave on Mount Sinai.

And if we were given that privilege we too would need to veil our faces so as not to frighten our companions. Words fail!

1 Corinthians 13: 19-20
When I was a child, I spoke as a child, I understood as a child, I thought as a child; but, when I became a man, I put away childish things. For now we see through a glass darkly, but then face to face; now I know in part, but then shall I know, even as also I am known.

The Fifth and final Principle.   *There is a constant action that employs all the powers of the new body and soul in order to enjoy God.*

Does it surprise you, Christian, that life eternal is to know God and Jesus Christ – that to enjoy God the Father and his Son Jesus Christ is eternal life?

If you are fixed on the things of this Earth and you consult your flesh on this matter, you will not think much of the idea of knowing God.

1 John 5: 19-20
But we know that we are of God, and the whole world lieth in wickedness; and we know that the Son of God is come, and hath given us an understanding, that we may know him that is true; and we are in him that is true, even in his Son Jesus Christ. This is the true God and eternal life.

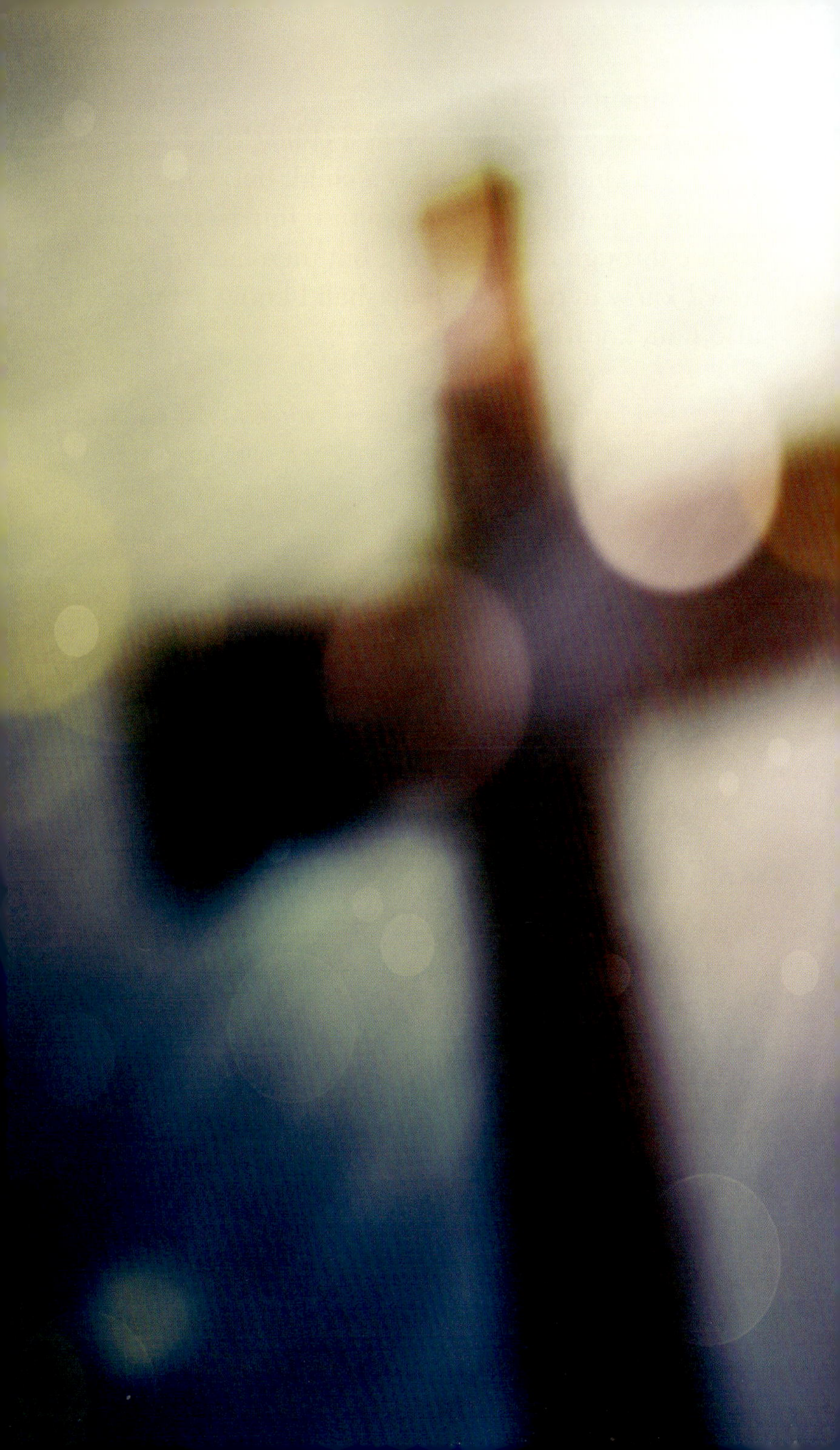

Chapter 9

Heaven – a place to remember

THE story is told of the man who woke every morning with no memory of anything that had happened in his life before the morning of his rising.

Some imagine that Heaven will be the land of forgetfulness. All memory of past sins and failures gone. All memories that would cause pain vanquished.

Is this your view of Heaven?

Yes, it is true that God remembers our sins no more. We who have been washed clean by the precious blood of the Savior need not fear the wrath of God. He has removed our sins as far from us as the east is from the west.

But your memory will not be idle, or useless, in the everlasting rest. It will be a heightened memory that can now look behind Him and before Him. It will be a memory ever ready to compare past things with present things.

But instead of bringing sorrow and condemnation this capacity for memory will lift the soul up to bless the Lord and be filled with inconceivable esteem as we consider our heavenly condition.

To stand on that mount like Moses and see at the same time the wilderness in which 38 long years of discipline weighed heavy on the soul and the Promised Land – then how much better to stand in Heaven and look back on Earth, and weigh them together in the balance.

Will this not cause the soul to cry out with wonder as it considers the gale force grace that blew us into the safe harbor rest of Heaven?

Will not the soul consider it and wonder at the cost of the transport? Was it not the most costly of trips, bought by the blood of Christ?

Memory! Oh yes, you will remember. And with each remembrance the soul will be lifted up and swept over with unspeakable love and gratitude that can no longer be contained. Heaven will be full of the praise of the redeemed.

Think of it, Christian. Your presence and place in Heaven was why Christ sought you with his tender alluring love. This is the blessed end of all that went before. This is what the Scriptures spoke of, the ministers preached, the evangelist beckoned. This puts an end to all the sad tiding our souls have borne here on Earth, all the humbling and correction that caused such discouragement, all the failures that caused us such misery and sorrow.

You will finally fully appreciate the Gospel and apprehend the good tidings – of peace, goodness, and joy. Finished are the bitter mourning, fasting and heaviness of heart.

> Is my praying, watching, and fearing to offend come to this?

> Are all my afflictions, Satan's temptations, the world's scorns and jeers, come to this?

> Is this what my vile nature resisted for so long?

> Is this the place that my unworthy soul has come to so unwillingly?

> Was the world too good to lose for this? Were all the wearisome duties of being a Christian to large a price for this?

The day will come, dear Saint, when your soul will query you and ask, could we not have left all for this? Could not we suffer anything for this? Could not even life itself have been forfeited for this?

Oh yes, my friend, the day will come when you will

but the greatest of these is love."

Let us think for just a moment on this one thing that remains that is above all others. Yes, faith is present in heaven. Yes, hope is present in heaven. And these are tantalizing truths. But let's focus on the one surviving attribute that is above all others, *love!*

And what will be the sweet enjoyment of the saint's everlasting rest? Is it not love? The scriptures teach:

> Ephesians 3:19
> And to know the love of Christ, which passeth knowledge, that ye might be filled with all the fulness of God.

> John 4:16
> And we have known and believed the love that God hath to us. God is love; and he that dwelleth in love dwelleth in God, and God in him.

First let's look at knowledge and love as co-revelators that are connected to each other. Simply put, the scriptures teach that there is a direct correlation between knowing and loving God.

To know little of Christ is to love Him with only the smallest part of your heart. To have explored little of His kindness leaves the soul anemic with pounds of complaints and only ounces of love. To have spent next to no time at all viewing the gracious works of

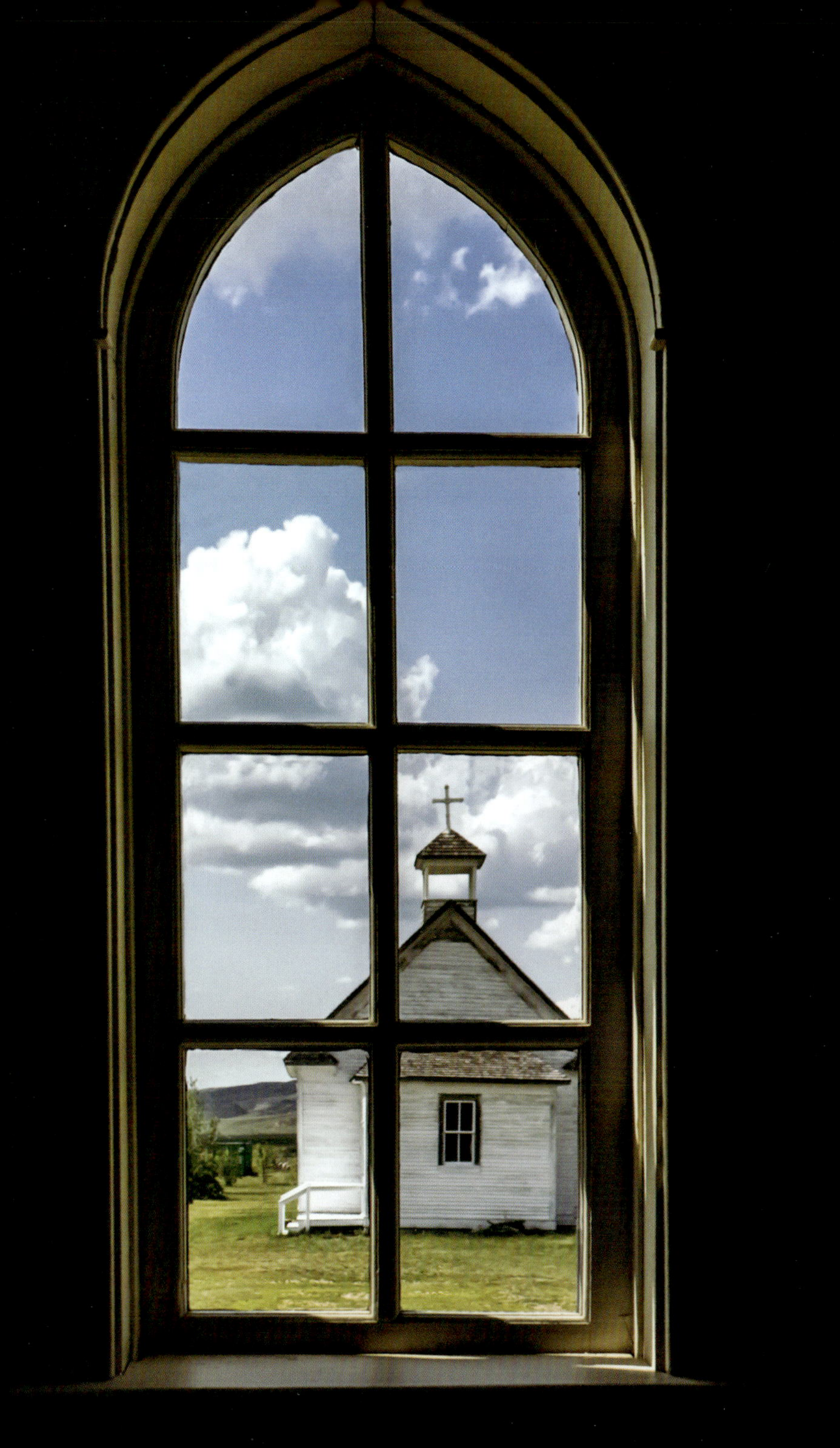

the Savior will produce in the heart a paltry portion of love. To have sparingly considered all the experiences of His love toward you, will leave you with a frozen heart incapable of experiencing the divine sunshine of His goodness.

> God loved you when you were his enemy. – when you knew nothing of Him, and cared even less.
>
> When you filled your cup with sin and rebellion, He overfilled His cup with love for you.
>
> When you shunned Him, He embraced you.

But make no mistake about this love; it is not a theoretical, but a practical love. It is a love that always affects its object in four important ways.

And if any of these four are missing, then so is love. Without God's love you are eternally lost.

> First, it is a love that draws the sinner to the Savior.
>
> Second, it is a love that produces in the sinner a love for the Savior.
>
> Third, it is a love that both redeems and transforms the sinner into a saint.
>
> Fourth, it is a love that transports the redeemed saint to an everlasting rest.

Does your soul desire to love Christ more? Good. This is the heavenly seed planted by the Spirit of God within your very soul. This is the one growing thing in you that should require your attention above all else. The health and wellbeing of this flower should be the focus of your attention. You should be constantly vigilant to see that it is well watered and tended.

The tender blossoms of this most precious flower must be guarded and never neglected. And here is the reason why:

> Your enjoyment of the saints everlasting rest will be increased or diminished based on how much your soul loves the Savior.

My ancestor ten generations back was William Penn, who wrote the book *No Cross No Crown*. This is a book worth reading, as it is full of Gospel truth. One of the points Penn made was that without performing the *duties* laid upon us by a good confession of the Gospel of Jesus Christ, there is no *reward*.

While I would never want to distract from the simple truth that there is a cost associated with discipleship to Jesus – a cost that, once embraced, will produce an eternal crown in glory – let me add some needed texture to this truth.

Discipleship will not on its own produce a crown, or even entrance into Heaven, if that discipleship is not

charged at its very core by a love for the Savior.
Jesus said:

> John 14:15
> If you love me, keep my commandments.
>
> John 14:21
> And again he said, He that hath my commandments, and keepeth them, he it is that loveth me: and he that loveth me shall be loved of my Father, and I will love him, and will manifest myself to him.

Notice what Jesus is *not* saying. He is not saying that keeping his commandments produces love for Him. Just the opposite is true. Jesus is pointing out the extraordinary nexus between loving Him and what happens next. Duty follows love, not the other way around.

Duty without love for the Savior may produce its own rewards and some wonderful benefits, but the saint's everlasting rest is not one of them. So let me propose that the source of our crowns is not bearing our own cross, but coming to grips with the reality of the Savior's cross.

- It is at His cross that you meet yourself as you really are.
- It is at His cross that you see your sin for what it really is.

- It is at His cross that you come to realize that everything you thought was praiseworthy about yourself is but vanity.
- It is at His cross that you begin the journey that leads to an utter rejection of your own merits.
- It is at His cross that you despair of any and all personal means to change the downward direction of your soul.
- It is at His cross that your fate is fixed and you see that your present course is doomed to destruction.
- It is at His cross that you lose all hope in self.
- It is at His cross that the sins once gloried are now shunned and shameful.

Much more could be recited, but it is enough to summarize that it is at His cross that the hideous truth about yourself and your horrible fate are revealed without compromise or excuse.

And once these visions of reality take hold you will find something most unexpected also at the cross. It is at the cross, and only at the cross, that you will find God loving you through the bloody sacrifice of His own precious Son.

Could you make your way to the foot of the cross of Jesus? And for some let me say, if you do not need cleansing than do not look up.

If you do not need forgiveness for the myriad of sins you have knowingly committed and the tens of thousands of which you are blissfully unaware, then do not look up.

If you think you can make it to the safe harbor of Heaven on your own merits, then do no look up.

If you doubt the love of God and see the death of Jesus as simply a sad moment in history, do not look up.

If you do not wish to be delivered from the bondage of your heart and mind that is at constant warfare with the laws of God, then do not look up.

In a word, if you do not understand, feel or see your great need to be rescued, then by all means do not look up.

For the rest of you who are perishing and know it, and have despaired of any hope, I invite you to look up and see the provision that has been made for your complete salvation and restoration.

Some move too quickly from the cross and in so doing miss many of the crowns that have been laid up in Heaven for those who make the foot of the cross their home away from home. And here the mystery of the saint's everlasting rest begins to unfold.

Pay attention if you seek crowns in Heaven, as you are about to discover one of the most profound truths ever revealed regarding your enjoyment of Heaven.

We have been hinting at it, and now we will unfold it all and lay it before your soul for full examination.

Earlier in this book, I made the following statement:

> The most happiness that can ever be attained is found in the rest promised by our Lord. It is by way of description the perfect and endless enjoyment of God by those saints who have been perfected by God. And the enjoyment they receive will be according to the measure of their capacity that is arrived at by their souls upon their death. An enjoyment to be realized fully after the resurrection of the dead and the final judgment.
> Or put another way. *Heaven will not be the same for all saints.*

It is with special attention that I would ask you to consider that the enjoyment you as a saint will receive will be according to the measure of your capacity that is arrived at by your soul at the moment of your death.

Now the question is: Capacity for what? What determines this capacity? My endless enjoyment of Heaven depends upon a capacity, so what determines how large the capacity?

Is it the good works done in the flesh? Is it my loyalty to the Lord and his Gospel? Is it the sacrifices I have made for the Gospel? Is it my perseverance as a saint? Is it my attention to Gospel duties? Is it my personal devotions? Is it my obedience to the commandments of Christ? I could go on.

The answer is that none of these things by themselves will determine your capacity to enjoy the saint's everlasting rest.

So what will?

It is your love for the Savior that will determine your capacity to enjoy Heaven. All the rest flows from that fount.

The question that follows is, how do I increase my love for the Savior?

First let me share with you *where* you increase your love for the Savior.

>Beneath the cross of Jesus!

Now let me share *how* you increase your love for the Savior.

>*Gratitude!*

Let me end this chapter with a summary of this revelation given through a story by the Lord Jesus Christ himself.

Luke 7:41-47

There was a certain creditor who had two debtors. One owed five hundred pence. The other owed fifty.
When they had nothing to pay, the creditor forgave them both.

Tell me therefore, which of them will love him most?
Simon answered and said, "I suppose he to whom he forgave most.

And Jesus said unto him, "Thou hast rightly judged."

And he turned to a woman, and said unto Simon, "Seest thou this woman? I entered into thine house, thou gavest me no water for my feet. But she hath washed my feet with tears, and wiped them with the hairs of her head.

"Thou gavest me no kiss: but this woman since the time I came in hath not ceased to kiss my feet.

"My head with oil thou didst not anoint, but this woman hath anointed my feet with ointment.

Wherefore I say unto thee, her sins, which are many, are forgiven; for she loved much: but to whom little is forgiven, the same loveth little.

And now you know the secret to increasing your enjoyment of the saint's everlasting rest.

I would encourage you to go to the the cross of Jesus and spend the rest of your life increasing your capacity to enjoy Heaven.

It is only at the cross that you can begin to plumb the depths of your sin and it is only at the cross that you can begin to fathom the love of Jesus for sinners such as yourself.

Increase your gratitude for the Savior and your love for him will grow, as is fitting a right in the sight of God.

Shadow of a Wooden Cross

The shadow of a wooden cross,
 A rising Son displayed;
On that spot and on that day
 An ancient debt was paid.

Prophetic WORD, merged with flesh,
 With love bound to a tree;
There Justice met with Mercy
 For all the world to see.

Divine the name of He Who hangs
 With emblem wounds of glory;
Page of light that turned the night
 Into another story.

Joy was mixed with agony
 That day upon the tree;
Reflecting on the Book of Life,
 My Savior thought of me.

– CJ Lovik

About the Author

C. J. Lovik graduated from Westmont College California with a degree in Education and Communication. He taught elementary school in Southern California.

After teaching and writing children's books for many years, he started a manufacturing business and developed an online family-friendly internet search engine.

He is the author of *The Living Word in 3D* book series, which explores a revelatory code embedded into the Book of Genesis that anticipates the coming of Christ.

An edited and updated version of John Bunyan's classic, The Pilgrim's Progress: From This World to That Which Is to Come, published in 2009, was C.J.'s first book for adults.

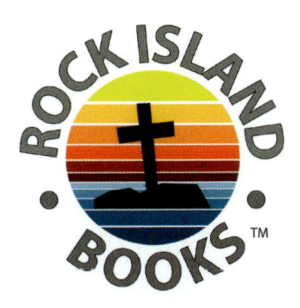

www.rockislandbooks.com
Visit our website to purchase books and preview upcoming titles.

Contact us at:
books@rockisland.com